HOW TO CONDUCT SURVEYS

SECOND EDITION

This book is dedicated to the ones I love:

John C. Beck and Ingrid, Anja, and Astrid.

HOW TO CONDUCT SURVEYS

A STEP-BY-STEP GUIDE

SECOND EDITION

ARLENE FINK
JACQUELINE KOSECOFF

SAGE Publications
International Educational and Professional Publisher
Thousand Oaks   London   New Delhi

For information:

  SAGE Publications, Inc.
2455 Teller Road
Thousand Oaks, California 91320
E-mail: order@sagepub.com

SAGE Publications Ltd.
6 Bonhill Street
London EC2A 4PU
United Kingdom

SAGE Publications India Pvt. Ltd.
M-32 Market
Greater Kailash I
New Delhi 110 048 India

Printed in the United States of America

Library of Congress Cataloging-in-Publication Data

Fink, Arlene.
    How to conduct surveys: A step-by-step guide / by Arlene Fink and
Jacqueline Kosecoff. — 2nd ed.
        p.   cm.
    Includes bibliographical references and index.
    ISBN 0-7619-1408-0 (cloth: acid-free paper). —
    ISBN 0-7619-1409-9 (pbk.: acid-free paper)
    1. Social surveys.   2. Educational surveys.   I. Kosecoff,
Jacqueline B.   II. Title
    HN29.F53   1998
    300′.723—dc21   97-45246

98 99 00 01 02 03 10 9 8 7 6 5 4 3 2

Acquiring Editor:	C. Deborah Laughton
Editorial Assistant:	Eileen Carr
Production Editor:	Diana E. Axelsen
Production Assistant:	Denise Santoyo
Typesetter/Designer:	Janelle LeMaster
Indexer:	Virgil Diodato
Cover Designer:	Ravi Balasuriya
Print Buyer:	Anna Chin

CONTENTS

PREFACE

The second edition of this book shares the same goal as the first: to guide readers in developing their own rigorous surveys and evaluating the credibility of other ones. Like the first edition, this one also gives practical step-by-step advice on how to achieve the goal. But most of the similarities end here.

We have completely revised this second edition to reflect changes in the way people prepare surveys, use them with the public, and report the results. You will find that this book now covers computer-assisted and interactive surveys. We ask and answer questions such as, How do computer-based surveys compare in uses, outcomes, and costs with more traditional survey methods such as telephone interviews and mailed questionnaires? Does new technology mean better surveys? We also discuss methods of ensuring that the survey sample you plan to assemble—regardless of the type of survey—will be large enough to detect a difference between groups (if one exists).

Surveys, which are used in nearly every setting from business to the arts, have come under increasing scrutiny for possible violations of privacy. To help you with that hurdle, this second edition provides guidelines for preparing informed consent statements for survey respondents and for asking them sensitive questions about ethnicity, income, and gender. In recent years, we have also recognized the need for translating surveys—even small ones—into other languages, and this edition of the book provides step-by-step advice on how to ensure that your translation gets you the information you need.

This new edition teaches you how to read computer output containing survey results and provides access to new survey data analysis techniques such as odds rations, relative risks, and confidence intervals. We also provide guidelines for preparing reports, including written structured abstracts (a new way of summarizing survey purposes, methods, and finding), and for giving oral presentations using overheads and slides.

We have geared the book for everyone who needs to learn how to do a survey, regardless of their statistical background. We have added numerous examples to the book, added new exercises (and answers), and provided new appendixes with rules for performing technical computations. We think the book is useful for self-learning and in workshops, seminars, and formal classrooms.

We are perpetually grateful to Drs. David Kanouse and Wendy Everett Watson, who advised us on the first edition. For the second edition, we still thank the clan whose number has grown substantially. We are also grateful to the Sage team. (We have to stop meeting like this.) Specifically, we thank Diana Axelsen, the production editor; Janelle LeMaster, who did the interior design and typesetting; Kate Peterson, the copy editor; Ravi Balasuriya, who did the cover; and Eileen Carr, the editorial assistant.

Special heartfelt thanks go to C. Deborah Laughton, who is an editor, a best friend, and just the best! Nothing would get done without her patience, perseverance, and impeccable manners. They don't come any better.

CONDUCTING SURVEYS
Everyone Is Doing It

OVERVIEW

A survey is a method of collecting information from people about their ideas, feelings, health, plans, beliefs, and social, educational, and financial background. It usually takes the form of self-administered questionnaires and interviews. Self-administered questionnaires can be completed by hand (paper-and-pencil) or by computer. Interviews take place in person (face-to-face) or on the telephone. Used to help policymakers, program planners, evaluators, and researchers, surveys are most appropriate when information should come directly from people.

All surveys rely on directly asking people questions to get information. Surveys must be concerned with who and how many will be asked questions (sampling), when and how often (design), and processing, analysis, and interpretation of data. Pilot testing helps get all survey methods in shape and can even help boost the response rate.

To choose among survey types (questionnaires or interviews) or methods of administration (mail, telephone, or computer), select one that is credible and for which you have resources.

Survey purposes and methods fall on a continuum. Some surveys can have far-reaching, generalizable effects, and their methods must be scientific. Others are conducted to meet very specific needs; their methods may not always achieve scientific rigor, but they must still be accurate.

WHAT IS A SURVEY?

A survey is a method of collecting information directly from people about their ideas, feelings, health, plans, beliefs, and social, educational, and financial background. A survey can be a self-administered questionnaire that someone fills out alone or with assistance. Or a survey can be an interview that is done in person or on the telephone.

Some surveys are on paper or disk and the respondent can complete them privately at home or in a central location, say, at a health center. The respondent can either return the completed survey on the disk or mail the responses electronically. Surveys can also be interactive, requiring a telephone or cable connection. Interactive surveys guide the re-

spondent through the survey and provide audio and visual cues to help. Interviews may be conducted with or without the aid of a computer.

There are at least three good reasons for conducting surveys:

Reason 1: *A policy needs to be set or a program must be planned.*

Examples: Surveys to Meet Policy or Program Needs

- The YMC Corporation wants to determine which hours to be open each day. The corporation surveys employees to find out which eight-hour shifts they are willing to work.
- The national office of the Health Voluntary Agency is considering providing day care for the children of its staff.

How many have very young children? How many would use the agency's facility?

- Ten years ago, the Bartley School District changed its language arts curriculum. Since then, some people have argued that the curriculum has become out of date. What do the English teachers think? If revisions are needed, what should they look like?

Reason 2: *You want to evaluate the effectiveness of programs to change people's knowledge, attitudes, health, or welfare.*

Examples: Surveys in Evaluations of Programs

- The YMC Corporation has created two programs to educate people about the advantages and disadvantages of working at unusual hours. One program takes the form of individual counseling and a specially prepared, self-monitored videotape. The second program is conducted in large groups. A survey is conducted six months after each program is completed to find out if the employees think they got the information they needed. The survey also aims to find out if they would recommend that others participate in a similar program and how satisfied they are with their work schedule.
- The Health Voluntary Agency is trying two approaches to child care. One is primarily "child centered," and the children usually decide what they would like to do during the hours they are in the program. The other is academic and artistic. Children are taught to read, play musical instruments, and dance at set times during the day. Which program is most satisfactory in that the parents, children, and staff are active participants and pleased with the curriculum's content?
- The Bartley School District changed its language arts curriculum. A survey is conducted to find out whether and how the change has affected parents' and students' opinions of the high school program.

Reason 3: *You are a researcher and a survey is used to assist you.*

Examples: Surveys for Research

- Because the YMC Corporation has so many educational programs, it wants to research how adults learn best. Do

they prefer self-learning or formal classes? Are reading materials appropriate or are films and videotapes better? How do they feel about computer-assisted learning or learning directly from the Internet? As part of their research, and to make sure all the possibilities are covered, the corporation conducts a survey of a sample of employees to learn their preferences.

- The Health Voluntary Agency is considering joining with a local university in a study of preschool education. The agency conducts a survey of the parents participating in the new day care programs. The survey asks about the participants' education and income. Researchers need data such as these so that they can test one of their major assumptions, namely, that parents with higher education and incomes are more likely to choose the less academic of the two preschool programs.
- The Bartley School District is part of a federally funded national study of the teaching of the English language. The study's researchers hypothesized that classroom teaching depends more on the teachers' educational backgrounds and reading preferences than on the formal curriculum. A survey is conducted to find out teachers' educational backgrounds and reading habits so those data are available for testing the researchers' hypothesis.

WHEN IS A SURVEY BEST?

Many methods are available for obtaining information about people. A survey is only one. Consider the youth center whose major aim is to provide a variety of services to the community. It offers medical, financial, legal, and educational assistance to residents of the city who are between 12 and 21 years of age regardless of economic or ethnic background. The program is particularly proud of its coordinated approach, arguing that the center's effectiveness comes from making available many services in one location to all participants. Now that the center is ten years old, a survey is to be conducted to find out just how successful it really is. Are participants and staff satisfied? What services do young people use? Is the center really a multiservice one? Are people better off with their health and other needs because of their participation in the center? A mailed, self-administered questionnaire survey is decided on to help answer these and other questions. Here are some excerpts from the questionnaire:

Examples: Excerpts From an Overly Ambitious Self-Administered Questionnaire

5. Is your blood pressure now normal?   *11*

      Yes   1
      No   2

7. Which of the following social services have you used in the past year?
   (Please indicate yes or no for each service.)   *15-18*

Services	Yes	No
Medical	1	2
Legal	1	2
Financial	1	2
Educational	1	2

10. Check how satisfied you are with each of the following services   *20-28*

Services	Definitely satisfied	Satisfied	Neither satisfied nor dissatisfied	Not Satisfied	Definitely not satisfied
Daily counseling session	1	2	3	4	5
Legal aid facility	1	2	3	4	5
Library	1	2	3	4	5

11. How much time in a five-minute period does the doctor spend
   listening (rather than, say, talking) to you? (Please check one)   *29*

_____ Less than one minute
_____ About one or two minutes
_____ More than two minutes

The questionnaire was shown to a reviewer, whose advice was to eliminate Questions 5, 7, and 11, and keep only Question 10. The reviewer stated that surveys are not best for certain types of information. Here's the reasoning:

Question 5 asks for a report of a person's blood pressure. Is it normal? In general, information of this kind can best be obtained from other sources, such as medical records or directly from a doctor. Many people might have difficulty recalling their blood pressure with precision and also would be at a loss to define "normal" blood pressure.

Question 7 may be all right if you feel confident that the person's recall will be accurate. Otherwise, the records of the center (particularly if they are kept well) are probably a better source of information about which services are used.

Question 11 asks for how much time the doctor spends with the patient. Unless you are interested in a study of perceptions of time spent between doctor and patient, probably the best way to get this information is through observation.

Question 10 is appropriate. Only participants can tell you how satisfied they are. No other source will do as well.

Surveys are by no means the only source of information for policymakers, evaluators, or researchers, nor are they necessarily the most relevant. Some other sources of information are the following:

- Observations or eyewitness accounts
- Performance tests that require a person to perform a task (such as teaching a lesson to a class); observers assess the effectiveness
- Written tests of ability or knowledge
- Record reviews that rely on existing documentation, such as reviews of medical records in physicians' offices and hospitals and school attendance records

Surveys can be used to make policy or to plan and evaluate programs and conduct research when the information you need should come directly from people. The data they provide are descriptions of attitudes, values, habits, and background characteristics such as age, health, education, and income.

Sometimes, surveys are used with other sources of information. This is particularly true for evaluations and research.

Example: Surveys Combined With Other Information Sources

- As part of its evaluation of child care programs, the Health Voluntary Agency surveyed parents, children, and staff about their degree of participation and satisfaction. Also, the agency reviewed financial records to evaluate the costs of each program, and standardized tests were given to appraise how ready children were for school.
- The YMC Corporation is researching how adults learn. Achievement and performance tests are given at regular intervals. In addition, a survey provides supplemental data on how adults like to learn.

QUESTIONNAIRES AND INTERVIEWS: THE HEART OF THE MATTER

All surveys consist of (1) questions and (2) instructions, and they make sense only in the context of (3) sampling and design, (4) data processing and analysis, (5) pilot testing, (6) response rate, and (7) reporting results.

Questions

Information from surveys is obtained by asking questions (sometimes called *items*). The questions may have forced response choices:

Example: Forced-Choice Item

What is the main advantage of using multiple-choice questions rather than essay questions in surveys?

_____ Can be scored quickly and objectively
_____ Are best at measuring complex behaviors
_____ Can have more than one right answer
_____ Are the least threatening of the question types

Questions on questionnaires or in interviews may be open ended.

Example: Open-Ended Item

What is the main advantage of using multiple-choice questions rather than essay questions for surveys?

Answer here:

The selection, wording, and ordering of questions and answers require careful thought and a reasonable command of language.

Instructions

Surveys always contain instructions for completion. Are all respondents to answer all questions? Is there a time limit? Must all questions be answered? In a survey of viewers' television habits,

one section—for example, asking for the programs watched regularly—may be mandatory, whereas a second—calling for demographic or background information on age, educational level, and income—may be optional.

Survey Sample and Design

Surveys are data collection techniques used to obtain information from people. From which people, how often, and when? As soon as you raise such questions, you must become concerned with the sample and design of the survey. The *sample* is the number of people in the survey. The *design* often refers to when the survey takes place (just once, or cross-sectional; over time, or longitudinal). Consider these survey questions:

- Survey Question 1:
  What do college graduates know about physical fitness?
  Design: Cross-sectional
  Sample: Graduates from State College's class of 1998
  Method: Mailed, self-administered questionnaire

- Survey Question 2:
  What do college graduates know about physical fitness?
  Sample: Graduates from State College's classes of 1998, 1999, and 2000
  Design: Longitudinal
  Method: Mailed, self-administered questionnaire

- Survey Question 3:
  How has college graduates' knowledge of physical fitness changed over time?
  Sample: Graduates from the class of 1998 surveyed in 1998, 2003, and 2008
  Design: Longitudinal
  Method: Mailed, self-administered questionnaire

Question 1 asks for a portrait of the class of 1998's knowledge of physical fitness, and a mailed questionnaire is to be used. But must all graduates be included in the portrait? If only a sample is chosen, the survey will take less time and cost less. But will those in the sample think like everyone else? Fortunately, strategies exist for making sure that the sample is a microcosm of all graduates. If 40% of the 1998 graduates are male and, of that, 10% are Hispanic, you can draw a sample that reflects these proportions. The sample will be large enough to be meaningful, but not so large as to break the bank.

If the graduating class of 1998 contains only 100 people, and you can afford to survey all of them, then you do not have to worry about sampling. You will, however, be concerned with the fact that the survey is using a *cross-sectional* design in which people are surveyed just once. This is different from a *longitudinal* design in which people are surveyed more often. Question 2 calls for a longitudinal design because data are being collected from three graduating classes. To answer the questions about what graduates know about physical fitness, the three classes' answers can be compared or combined.

The third question calls for surveys over a five-year period and also uses a longitudinal design. In this case, however, the sample consists of students from just one graduating class and the survey is to describe how their knowledge of fitness changed.

All three surveys rely on mailed, self-administered questionnaires, but their designs and samples vary.

Planning for Data Analysis

Regardless of your survey's size, you must think ahead to how you plan to analyze the survey's data.

Will you compute percentages so that your results look like this?

> Of the total sample, 50% reported that they were Republicans; 42%, Democrats; 4%, socialists; 1% belonged to the Green Party; and 3% had no party affiliation.

Will you produce averages to appear this way?

> The average age of the respondents is 56.4 years. The median educational level is 13 years.

Will you compare groups?

> A total of 60% of the men, but only 20% of the women, were Republicans.

> Respondents do not differ significantly in satisfaction with the present government.

Will you look for relationships such as this?

> The survey found no connection between how liberal or conservative people were and their educational attainments.

Will you look for changes over time?

> Since 1997, statistically significant differences have been found in the number of men participating in two or more hours of child care per day.

Pilot Testing

A pilot test is a tryout, and its purpose is to help produce a survey form that is usable and that will provide you with the information you need. All types of questionnaires and interviews must be pilot tested. Self-administered questionnaires are heavily dependent on the clarity of their language, and pilot testing quickly reveals whether people understand the directions you have provided and if they can answer the questions. A pilot test of a face-to-face interview will also tell you about interviewers. Can they follow the form easily? Are the spaces large enough for recording responses? Pilot tests can also tell you how much time it takes to complete the survey.

Testing helps make the survey run smoothly. Whenever possible, you should try to duplicate the environment in which the survey is to take place. That might mean obtaining permission from people to be in the tryouts, but not in the survey, even though they are eligible for full participation.

Response Rate

The surveyor wants everyone who is eligible to respond to all questions. Pilot testing helps improve the response rate because it can eliminate severe potential sources of difficulty such as poorly worded questions and no place to record answers. Furthermore, if the entire set of survey procedures is carefully tested, then this, too, can help the response rate. Before you do a telephone interview, ask: Do you have available a current source of information on people's telephone numbers? Are you willing to make telephone calls at the time the survey respondents are available? Other ways of ensuring good response rates exist. Among them are keeping surveys short and providing incentives (such as payment for participating).

How high should the response rate be? If you are conducting a large, complex survey, you will want to use statistical procedures to answer this question. If your survey is relatively simple (e.g., a pool of teachers in a school or nurses in three hospitals), then you have to decide how many people you will need for the results to be believable. If there are 20 people who are eligible for completing a mailed, self-administered questionnaire and only 10 respond, you may feel different from the way you will feel if, at another time, 200 out of 400 respond. Both surveys have a 50% response rate, but reporting on the views of 10 out of 20 people may appear less convincing than of 200 out of 400. Except when done statistically, the desired response rate tends to be entirely subjective and the general rule is "higher is better."

Reporting Results

Survey results are reported daily on television and in the newspaper. To much of the public, a survey is a poll, usually of some, but not all, people about an issue of immediate political, social, or economic concern. Survey results typically look like this:

Example 1: The Look of Survey Results

Question: If the election were held today, would you vote for Candidate X?

Answer: Of the men, 125 of 132 (94.6%) responded. Of the women, 200 of 210 (95.2%) responded. The results are given here in percentages.

	Yes	No	Don't Know
Men	62	18	20
Women	10	85	5

Example 2: The Look of Survey Results

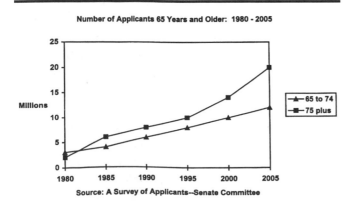

Number of Applicants 65 Years and Older: 1980 - 2005

Source: A Survey of Applicants--Senate Committee

To get results such as these requires many steps, and all surveys follow them:

- Deciding on the type of survey (mailed questionnaire, telephone, or face-to-face interviews)
- Selecting the survey's content, writing questions, and trying out the form
- Deciding who should participate (everyone? a sample of people?) and when (just once? each year for five years?)
- Administering the survey (Who should conduct the interview? By when must the questionnaire be returned?)
- Processing, analyzing, and interpreting the results (Did enough people participate? What do the numbers or differences mean? Just how do people feel about Candidate X? Have opinions changed over time?)
- Reporting the results orally or in writing in charts, tables, or graphs

No credible survey can omit any single step, although, depending on its purposes and resources, some steps will receive more emphasis in any given survey than in another.

Survey Types: The Friendly Competition

How do you choose between self-administered questionnaires and interviews? Is a mailed questionnaire better than a telephone interview? When are computer-based surveys best? Here are some criteria for selecting among the different survey types.

Reliability and Validity. A *reliable* survey results in consistent information. A *valid* survey produces accurate information. Reliable and valid surveys are obtained by making sure the definitions and models you use to select questions are grounded in theory or experience. No single survey type starts out with better reliability and validity. Choose the method that is most precise and accurate for your specific purposes. For example, if you are worried that the people you are surveying cannot read well, an oral interview or a computer-assisted survey is likely to produce better results. Focus groups and pilot tests help you decide which type to use and if you have done a good job of designing the survey and making it user-friendly. Respondents or administrators who have trouble with the survey will use it incorrectly, introducing bias that reduces the accuracy of the results. A well-designed, easy-to-use survey always contributes to reliability and validity.

Usefulness or Credibility of Results. The results will be useful if they are valid and if the survey device is one that users accept as the correct one. Find out before you start which method is the one people want. Sometimes the people who will use the results have strong preferences.

Costs. This refers to the financial burden of using the instrument. The costs associated with written (on-site and mailed) questionnaires include paper, reproduction, and incentives. Mailed questionnaires require an up-to-date address list (which you may have to purchase), postage, and envelopes. Sometimes you have several follow-up mailings, adding to the costs.

The costs of face-to-face and telephone interviews (not computerized) include purchasing a telephone system and paying for miscalled and out-of-date telephone numbers. You also need to pay for writing a script for the interviewer, training the interviewers, monitoring the quality of the interviews, and providing incentives.

Computer-based surveys require extensive development and testing. Any mistakes in programming or analysis can invalidate the survey's findings. Unless you have the skills and resources, it is best to rely on other people's surveys—assuming that they are valid for your purposes. Costs mount if you need to purchase computers. Interactive surveys require special programming expertise, access to special networks (like the Internet) at the place of administration, and special methods of ensuring confidentiality. Also, for some time to come, certain respondents (such as some who have not grown up with computers, or those who prefer to take cyberspace slowly) will continue to mistrust computers and computer-based surveys. Computers also sometimes fail.

Confidentiality. To preserve confidentiality, you code all forms and keep them in a secured place. Once the data are entered, you can destroy the originals. If the surveys are Web based, they will have an encrypted method of destroying names.

Table 1.1 compares the advantages and disadvantages of the major survey types and reminds you of their special needs and costs.

A SURVEY CONTINUUM: FROM SPECIFIC TO GENERAL USE

Surveys have become a major means of collecting data to answer questions about health and social, economic, and political life. How extensive and scientific must a survey be?

Compare these two surveys:

Example: Survey With a Specific Use

The directors of the Neighborhood Halfway Houses want to provide services that are appropriate for residents. At present, many complaints have arisen over the lack of adequate fitness facilities. A survey will be conducted to poll the five health care providers, 100 residents, and ten full- and part-time staff to find out what facilities are desirable and affordable.

Example: Survey With a General Use

This County Health Department is concerned with the effectiveness of its ten halfway houses. Together, the ten houses have 20,000 residents and 220 full- and part-time staff. This County has negotiated arrangements for health care services from a number of providers in the public and private sectors. As part of its effectiveness study, This County is surveying a random sample of residents, staff, and providers at all houses. NextDoor County is interested in adopting This County's halfway house model and is anxiously waiting for the results of the survey and the evaluation.

The justification for the first survey is one halfway house's concern with its own needs. The reason for the second is This County's interest in the effectiveness of all its halfway houses. Also, Next Door County is interested in the survey's results. Survey 1, with its limited impact, can be relatively informal in its methods. Survey 2, on the other hand, must be rigorous in its sampling plan, questionnaire construction, and data analysis and interpretation. Survey 1 is concerned primarily with usefulness. Survey 2 is also concerned with validity and generalizability: If adapted in another place

TABLE 1.1 Survey Types

	Self-Administered				Interviews	
	Mailed	*On-Site Paper-and-Pencil or Disk*	*On-Disk (on-site or mailed)*	*Interactive*	*Telephone*	*In-Person*
Characteristics	Respondents use paper and pencil	Respondents use paper and pencil or respond directly into the computer	Respondent answers directly onto the computer disk	Respondent uses a computer that is linked into a network or the Internet	Can be done with a written script or be computer assisted	Can be done with a written script or be computer assisted
Advantages	Can reach large geographic areas	Information is obtained immediately If supervisor is present, confusing survey questions can be clarified as needed	Can reach large geographic areas Order of questions can be preprogrammed Only "legal" answers are accepted	Can reach the world almost instantly Can give respondent an explanation of unfamiliar words and help with difficult questions Data can be automatically entered and analyzed	Can explore answers with respondents Can assist respondent with unfamiliar words	Same as telephone
Disadvantages	Need motivated respondents to return survey Respondents must be able to read, see, and write	Limited to responses from just those who are on site or can get there Respondents must be able to read, see, and write	Computer may quit Respondent must be willing to use the computer to complete a survey	Need access to system (like Internet) Respondent must be willing to use the computer to complete the survey System can go down	Need trained interviewers Need to make sure respondent is home If using computer-assisted interviews, will need technical expertise to program them	Need trained interviewers Must find a suitable place to conduct interview
Special needs	Up-to-date address list Follow-up mailings Incentives	Space and privacy for respondent to complete the survey	Programmer	Software engineer or programmer	Up-to-date phone numbers Schedule for reaching respondents May need a sampling expert for random digit dialing	If on site, need space and privacy May be difficult or dangerous to go to person's home
Costs	Printing, paper, envelopes, stamps, incentives	Printing, paper, incentives, survey supervisor, and possibly space for respondent to work	Computer, programmer, incentives	Mainly technical (e.g., software engineer), incentives	Training, incentives, telephones and telephone charges, computers and technical expertise, sampling expert	Training, space, travel, incentives

(Next Door County), will This County's halfway house model be equally effective?

Each time you do a survey, you must evaluate where its purposes fall on a continuum that goes from specific to general use. All generalizable surveys must be conducted with rigor.

2

THE SURVEY FORM
Questions, Scales, and Appearance

OVERVIEW

To select the content of a survey, you have to define the attitude, belief, or idea being measured. For example, what is meant by fear? a liberal perspective? self-esteem? Also, ask, "What information do I need and must therefore make certain I will be collecting?" Choose content that people will give you because they remember the details and can and will give them to you.

Survey questions may be forced choice or open ended. Forced-choice questions with several choices are easier to score than are open-ended, short-answer, essay questions. Open-ended questions give respondents an opportunity to state a position in their own words; unfortunately, these words may be difficult to interpret.

When writing forced-choice or open-ended questions, use standard English; keep questions concrete and close to the respondents' experience; become aware of words, names, and views that might automatically bias your results; check your own biases; do not get too personal; and use a single thought in each question.

The responses to closed-ended questions can take the form of yes-no answers, checklists, and rating scales. Rating scales may be graphic, but often they ask respondents to make comparisons in the form of ranks (1 = top to 10 = bottom), orders (1 = definitely agree, 2 = agree, 3 = disagree, 4 = definitely disagree), or continuums (your age). The numerical values assigned to rating scales can be classified as nominal, ordinal, interval, or ratio (numerical). Each has characteristics that must be considered when you analyze the results of your survey.

Surveyors are most often interested in responses to individual items such as the number of people who will vote for Candidate X or how often women between 65 and 80 years of age visit a doctor in a three-month period. Sometimes they are concerned with a score on a group of items that collectively represent respondents' views, health status, or feelings. Making scores meaningful by proving that high scorers are truly different from low scorers requires knowledge of (additive) scaling methods. Three commonly used methods create differential (Thurstone), summated (Likert), and cumulative (Guttman) scales.

THE CONTENT IS THE MESSAGE

Once you have decided that a survey is the method you want to use to gather data, you must consider the content or topics it will include. This is a difficult task because any single survey can encompass hundreds (or more) of ideas. Deciding on a survey's content means setting the survey's boundaries so that you can write the correct questions.

Suppose you were the evaluator of a youth center and that your main task was to find out whether the program's objectives had been achieved. Say that one of the objectives was to raise young people's self-esteem by providing them with education, jobs, financial help, and medical and mental health assistance. Suppose also that you decide to survey the young program participants to find out about their self-esteem. How would you determine which content to include?

To select the content of a survey you have to define your terms and clarify what you need and can get from asking people about their views.

DEFINE THE TERMS

Many human attitudes and feelings, such as self-esteem, are subject to a range of definitions. Does self-esteem mean feeling good about oneself, and if so, what does feeling good mean? The surveyor can answer questions of meaning by reviewing what is known and published about a concept such as self-esteem, consulting with experts, or defining it for himself or herself. The problem with your own definition is that others may not be convinced of its validity. When using a theoretical concept such as self-esteem, it is probably best to adopt a respected point of view, and even, if possible, an already existing and tested survey form.

Of course, for many surveys you will not be measuring theoretical ideas, but even so, you must define your terms. Suppose you were assessing a community's needs for health services. The terms *needs* and *health services* would certainly require definition because you can define them with respect to the type and nature of services that are required (outpatient clinics? hospitals? home visits?) and how convenient (time of day when doctors should be available) or how continuous they should be (must the same doctor always be available?).

SELECT YOUR INFORMATION
NEEDS OR HYPOTHESES

Suppose two surveyors choose the same definition of self-esteem for their evaluation study of the youth center. Depending on the circumstances, Surveyor 1 might decide to focus on self-esteem in relation to feelings of general well-being, whereas

Surveyor 2 may be concerned with feelings of self-esteem only as they manifest themselves in school or at work. Certainly, Surveyors 1 and 2, with their different orientations, will be asking several different questions. The results will yield different kinds of information. Surveyor 1, with a concern for general self-esteem, may not even cover work or school and will not be able to provide data on these topics. Surveyor 2, with his or her special interests in school and work, probably will not provide information on participant self-esteem with respect to personal relationships. The messages revealed by each survey will clearly be different.

Say you are interested in whether participants in the youth center had their general self-esteem enhanced after two years' participation in the program and that you have defined your terms to conform to an accepted theory of adolescent personality. To make sure you get all the data you need, you must ask the question: What information do I want and must therefore make certain I will be collecting? Remember, if you do not ask for it, you cannot report it later!

Here are some typical questions that the evaluator of the youth center could ask:

1. Is there a relationship between general feelings of self-esteem and whether the participant is a boy or girl?
2. Does a participant's self-esteem differ depending on how long he or she has been in the program?

These two questions suggest that the survey must get data on three topics:

- General self-esteem
- Gender of participant
- Length of participation in the program

If any of these topics was omitted, the surveyor of the youth center could not answer the two evaluation questions. After all, in this case the survey is being done only for the evaluation.

MAKE SURE YOU CAN GET
THE INFORMATION YOU NEED

In some cases, people may be reluctant to reveal their views. The evaluator of the youth center might find, for example, that young people are sensitive to questions about their feelings. In other cases, potential survey respondents may simply be unable to answer. Suppose you wanted to ask participants who had been attending the youth center for about six months about their attitudes toward school just before entering the center's program. Many may have forgotten. This inability to answer is a major problem with accurately predicting voters' preferences in national elections. It usually takes time for people to settle on a candidate, and frequently, people legitimately change their opinions several times during a campaign. That is why the national polls keep producing results that differ among themselves and from one point in time to another.

If you cannot get the information you need, you should find an alternative source of data, remove the topic from the survey, or wait until you can appropriately ask the question in a survey format.

DO NOT ASK FOR INFORMATION UNLESS YOU CAN ACT ON IT

In a survey of a community's needs for health services, it would be unfair to have people rate their preference for a trauma center if the community is unable to support such a service. Remember that the content of a survey can affect respondents' views and expectations. Why raise hopes that you cannot or will not fulfill?

Once you have selected the content and set the survey's boundaries, your next task is to actually write the questions. Write more questions than you plan to use because several will probably be rejected as unsuitable. First drafts often have items for which everyone gives the same answer or no one gives any answer at all. Before deciding on the number of items, sequence of questions, and coding requirements, you must be sure that you cover the complete domain of content you have identified as important to the survey. You may want to keep a list such as the following one used by the surveyor of participant satisfaction with the youth center. As you can see, this survey will not cover staff sensitivity, but will focus instead on consideration, accessibility, and availability of services.

Example: Plan for Survey of Satisfaction With the Youth Center

Topic	Number of Questions
1. Staff sensitivity	
Counselor usually listens	◯
Counselor is available when needed	◯
Appointment staff courteous	◯
.	
.	
.	
2. Accessibility of services	
Hours are convenient	⊬⊢ᴛ
Public transportation	⊦⊥⊬ᴛ I
3. Consideration of participant's needs	
Translation assistance	⊬⊢ᴛ
Ease of getting appointments	⊦⊬ᴛ I
Waiting times	⊦⊥⊬ᴛ I
.	
.	
.	
10. Availability of needed services	
Medical	⊬⊢ᴛ ⊬⊢ᴛ
Educational	⊬⊢ᴛ ⊬⊢ᴛ II

WRITING ITEMS

Open-Ended and Forced-Choice Questions

Survey items may take the form of questions:

Example: Open-Ended Question

1. How courteous are the people who make your appointments?

_____

_____

_____

Or they may be worded as statements:

Example: Forced-Choice Question

Circle your agreement or disagreement with the following:

2. The people who make my appointments are courteous.

	Circle one
Definitely agree	1
Agree	2
Disagree	3
Definitely disagree	4

Sometimes survey items are open ended, meaning that the respondents agree to answer the question or respond to the statement in their own words. Question 1 is open ended. At other times, survey items force the respondent to choose from preselected alternatives as in Question 2.

The overwhelming majority of surveys rely on forced-choice or multiple-choice questions because they have proven themselves to be the more efficient and ultimately more reliable. Their efficiency comes from being easy to use, score, and code for analysis. Also, their reliability is enhanced because of the uniform data they provide because everyone responds in terms of the same options (agree or disagree, frequently or infrequently, etc.).

Open-ended questions can offer insight into why people believe the things they do, but interpreting them can be extremely difficult unless they are accompanied by an elaborate coding system and people are trained to classify the data they get within the system.

Consider these two answers to a question from a survey of participants in an elementary school teaching program.

Example: Open-Ended Question for Elementary School Teaching Program

Question: What were the three most useful parts of the program?

_____

_____

_____

Answers: Respondent A

Instructor's lectures
The field experience
Textbook

Respondent B

Instructor
Teaching in the classroom
The most useful part was the excellent atmosphere for learning provided by the program

It is not easy to compare A's and B's responses. Respondent B lists the instructor as useful. Does this mean that the instructor is a useful resource in general, and how does this compare with Respondent A's view that the instructor's lectures were useful? In other words, are A and B giving the same answer? Respondent A says the textbook was useful. If only one text was used in the program, then A and B gave the same answer. But because the two recorded responses are different, some guessing or interpretation of what is meant is necessary.

Respondent A and B each mentioned something that the other did not: field experience and learning atmosphere. If these were equally important, then they could be analyzed individually. But suppose neither was particularly significant from the perspective of the survey's users. Would they then be assigned to a category labeled something like "miscellaneous"? Categories called miscellaneous usually are assigned all the difficult responses, and before you know it, miscellaneous can become the largest category of all.

Although it may be relatively easy for a respondent to answer an open-ended question, analysis and interpretation are quite complicated. The following closed-ended question could have been used to obtain the same information with the added result of making the responses easy to interpret.

Example: Closed-Ended Question for Elementary School Teaching Program

Circle one

	Definitely Not Satisfied	Not Satisfied	Satisfied	Definitely Satisfied
a. The textbook, *Teaching in the Classroom*	4	3	2	1
b. The instructor's knowledge of subject matter	4	3	2	1
c. The practicality of lecture topics	4	3	2	1
d. The field experience	4	3	2	1
e. Other, specify	4	3	2	1

ORGANIZING RESPONSES TO OPEN-ENDED SURVEY ITEMS: DO YOU GET ANY SATISFACTION?

A very common use of a survey is to find out whether people are satisfied with a new product, service, or program. Their opinions provide important insights into why new ideas or ways of doing things do or do not get used.

One open-ended set of questions that is particularly appropriate for getting at satisfaction requires collecting information about what people like best (LB) about the product or service and what they like least (LL).

Here is how the LB/LL technique works:

Step 1: Listing the Good and Bad

Ask respondents to list what is good and what is bad. Always set a limit on the number of responses: "List at least one thing, but no more than three things, you liked best about the conference." If participants cannot come up with three responses, they can leave blank spaces or write "none." If they give more than three, you can keep or discard the extras, depending on the information you need.

Instead of asking about the conference as a whole, you may want to focus on some particular aspect: "List at least one thing, but no more than three things, you liked best about the workshops."

Step 2: Coding LB/LL Data

Once you have all the responses, the next step is to categorize and code them. To do this, you can create categories based on your review of the re-sponses, or you can create categories based on past experience with similar programs.

Try to keep the categories as precise as possible—that is, more categories rather than fewer—because it is easier to combine them later if necessary than it is to break them up.

Suppose these were typical answers participants gave to the question on what they liked least about the conference:

- Some people did all the talking.
- The instructor didn't always listen.
- I couldn't say anything without being interrupted.
- Too much noise and confusion.
- Some participants were ignored.
- The instructor didn't take control.
- I didn't get a chance to say anything.
- Smith and Jones were the only ones who talked.
- The instructor didn't seem to care.
- I couldn't hear myself think.

You might categorize and code these as follows:

Example LB/LL: Response Categories

	Code
Instructor didn't listen (ignored participants; didn't seem to care)	1
Some people monopolized discussion (did all the talking; couldn't say anything; Smith and Jones were the only ones who talked)	2
Disorderly environment (too much noise; instructor didn't take control; couldn't hear myself think)	3

Now match your codes and the responses:

Example LB/LL: Participant Responses

	Code
Participant A	
Instructor didn't always listen	1
I couldn't hear myself think	3
I couldn't say anything without being interrupted	2
Participant B	
Instructor didn't always listen	1
The instructor didn't take control when	
things got noisy	3
The instructor ignored some students	3
Participant C	
I didn't get a chance to say anything	2

To make sure you assigned the codes correctly, you may want to establish their reliability. Are they clear enough so that at least two raters would assign the same code for a given response?

Step 3: LB/LL Data

When you are satisfied about reliability, the next step is to count the number of responses for each code.

Here's how to do this for ten participants:

Example LB/LL: Number of Responses for Each Code

	Code			
Participant	1	2	3	Total
A	1	1	1	3
B	1		2	3
C		2	1	3
D		1	2	3
E		3		3
F		2	1	3
G		2	1	3
H		2	1	3
I		3	2	5
J		1		1
	2	17	11	30

Look at the number of responses in each category. The ten participants listed a total of 30 things they liked least about the small group discussion. Seventeen out of 30 (more than 50%) were assigned to the same category, code 2, and the surveyor could justly argue that, based on the data, what the participants tended to like least about the workshops was that some people monopolized the discussions and others did not get a chance to say anything.

Next count the number of participants whose answers were assigned to each code. For example, only Participants A and B gave answers that were coded 1.

Example LB/LL: Participants' Response Pattern

Code	No. of Participants Listing a Response Assigned to This Code	Which Participants?
1	2	A, B
2	9	All but B
3	8	All but E and J

Look at the number of participants whose responses fit each category. Because 8 or 9 of the 10 participants gave responses that fell into the same two categories (codes 2 and 3), their opinions probably represent those of the entire group. It is safe to add that participants also disliked the disorderly atmosphere that prevailed during the workshops. They complained that the noise made it hard to think clearly, and the instructor did not take control.

When respondents agree with one another, there will be only a few types of answers, and these will be listed by many people. If respondents disagree, many different kinds of answers will turn up on their lists, and only a few people (less than 10%) will be associated with each type.

Interpreting LB/LL data gets more complex when you have many participants and responses to categorize. Suppose, for example, you asked 100 participants to indicate which aspects of a health education program they liked best.

First, you must decide on your response categories and assign each one a code. Then try this:

1. Put the codes in rank order. That is, if the largest number of participants chose responses that are assigned to code 3, list code 3 first.
2. Calculate the percentage of students assigned to each code. If 40 out of 100 students made responses that were assigned a code of 3, then the calculation would be 40%.
3. Count the number of responses assigned to each code.
4. Calculate the percentage of responses assigned to each code. If 117 responses from a total of 400 were assigned to code 3, then 29.25% or 117/400 of responses were for code 3.
5. Calculate the cumulative percentage of responses by adding the percentages together: 29.25% plus 20.25% is 49.50%.

Here is a table that summarizes these steps with some hypothetical data:

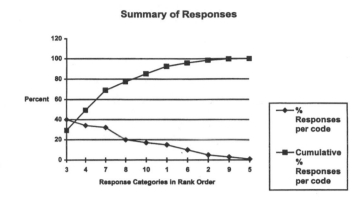

Figure 2.1. Summary of Responses

Example LB/LL: Summary of Responses

Response Categories (with codes in rank order)	% of Participants Assigned to Each Code (100 participants)	Number of Responses Assigned to Each Code (100 participants)	% of Responses Assigned to Each Code	Cumulative % Responses Assigned to Each Code
3	40	117	29.25	29.25
7	32	78	19.50	69.00
8	20	35	8.75	77.25
10	17	30	7.50	85.25
1	15	29	7.25	92.50
6	10	14	3.50	96.00
2	5	10	1.25	99.75
5	1	1	0.25	100.00

	3	4	7	8	10	1	6	2	9	5
% Responses per code	40	34	32	20	17	15	10	5	3	1
Cumulative % responses per code	29-25	49.5	69	77.25	85.25	92.5	96	98,5	99.75	100

You can then illustrate your findings graphically, as shown here:

As you can see, the response categories are rank ordered along the *x*-axis according to the number of participants assigned to each code. The *y*-axis represents percentages.

For each response category, you should look for two points on the *x*-axis: the percentage of participants and the cumulative percentage of responses. First, the cumulative percentages of responses are joined with a square (■). Next, some of the points representing percentages of participants are joined with a diamond (♦).

The graph shows that responses coded as 3, 4, and 7 seem to cluster together. They are the categories to be emphasized because the highest percentages of participants were assigned to these codes, and they account for a total of 69% of all responses.

Items 8, 10, and 1 form a second intuitive cluster that represents 23.5% of all responses. Taken together, responses coded as 3, 4, 7, 8, 10, and 1 account for 92.5% of the total.

RULES FOR WRITING SURVEY ITEMS WITH FORCED CHOICES

Multiple-choice, closed-ended survey questions consist of a stem, which presents a problem (typically in the form of a statement, question, brief case history, or situation), followed by several alternative choices or solutions. Here are rules for their construction.

1. *Each Question Should Be Meaningful to Respondents.* In a survey of political views, the ques-

tions should be about the political process, parties, candidates, and so on. If you introduce other questions that have no readily obvious purpose, such as those about age or gender, you might want to explain why they are being asked: "We are asking some personal questions so that we can look for connections between people's backgrounds and their views."

2. *Use Standard English.* Because you want an accurate answer to each survey item, you must use conventional grammar, spelling, and syntax. Avoid specialized words (unless you are testing people's knowledge of them) and abbreviations, and make sure that your items are not so lengthy that you are actually testing reading or vocabulary.

Example: Item-Writing Skills—Length, Clarity, Abbreviations, and Jargon

---

Length

Poor: The paucity of psychometric scales with high
             degrees of stability and construct validity is most
             bothersome to surveyors when measuring people's:
             1. Economic characteristics
             2. Feelings
             3. Knowledge
             4. Health

Better: The lack of reliable and valid methods causes sur-
             veyors the most problems when measuring people's:
             1. Economic characteristics
             2. Feelings
             3. Knowledge
             4. Health

Clarity

Poor: What remedy do you usually use for stomachaches?
Better: Which brand of medicine do you usually use for
             stomachaches?
Better: Do you usually use tablets or powder for stomach-
             aches?

Abbreviations

Poor: Which political party is responsible for the
             expanding size of the GDP?
             1. Republican
             2. Democrat

Better: Which political party is responsible for the
             expanding size of the gross domestic product?
             1. Republican
             2. Democrat

Jargon

Poor: In your view, which dyad is most responsible for
             feelings of trust in early childhood?
             1. Mother and father
             2. Father and sibling
             3. Mother and sibling

Better: In your view, which family combination is most
             responsible for feelings of trust in early childhood?
             1. Mother and father
             2. Father and sibling
             3. Mother and sibling

---

3. *Make Questions Concrete.* Questions should be close to the respondent's personal experience.

Example: Item-Writing Skills—Concrete Questions

Less concrete:	Did you enjoy the book?
More concrete:	Have you recommended the book to anyone else?
More concrete:	Have you read any other books by the same author?

Asking respondents if they enjoyed a book is more abstract than asking if they recommended it to others or read more books by the same author. The farther you remove a question from the respondent's direct experience, the closer you come to the problems associated with remembering.

Consider this:

Example: Item-Writing Skills—Specificity of Questions

A survey of attitudes toward hiring women for managerial positions in five companies was conducted in a small city. Among the questions asked was, "Do you think women have as good a chance as men for managerial positions?" A friend of the surveyor pointed out that a better way of asking the question was, "At (fill in name of company), do women have as good a chance as men for managerial positions?"

Be careful not to err on the concrete side. If you ask people how many hours of television they watched each day for the past week, you should be sure that no reason exists for believing that the past week was unusual so that the data would not be representative of a "true" week's worth of TV viewing. Among the factors that might affect viewers' habits are television specials such as the Olympics and cataclysms such as plane crashes, earthquakes, floods, and fires.

4. *Avoid Biased Words and Phrases.* Certain names, places, and views are emotionally charged. When included in a survey, they unfairly influence people's responses. Words such as *communist, president, George Washington, abortion,* and *alcoholic* are examples.

Suppose you were surveying people who had just been through a diet program. Which words should you use: *thin* or *slender; portly, heavy,* or *fat?*

Remember this?

I am firm.
You are stubborn.
He is a pig-headed fool.

Look at these questions.

Would you vote for Roger Fields?
Would you vote for Dr. Roger Fields?
Would you vote for Roger Fields, a liberal?

Although Roger Fields appears to be the most neutral description of the candidate, it may be con-

sidered the least informative. Yet the introduction of *Dr.* or *liberal* may bias the responses.

5. *Check Your Own Biases.* An additional source of bias is present when survey writers are unaware of their own position toward a topic. Look at this:

Example: Item-Writing Skills—Hidden Biases

Poor: Do you think the liberals and conservatives will soon reach a greater degree of understanding?

Poor: Do you think the liberals and conservatives will continue their present poor level of understanding?

When you are asking questions that you suspect encourage strong views on either side, it is helpful to have them reviewed. Ask your reviewer if the wording is unbiased and acceptable to persons holding contrary opinions. For a survey of people's views on the relationship between the liberals and the conservatives, you might ask:

Example: Item-Writing Skills—Hidden Biases

Better: In your opinion, in the next four years, how is the relationship between the liberals and the conservatives likely to change?
　　　Much improvement
　　　Some improvement
　　　Some worsening
　　　Much worsening
　　　Impossible to predict

---

6. *Use Caution When Asking About the Personal.* Another source of bias may result from questions that may intimidate the respondent. Questions such as "How much do you earn each year?" "Are you single or divorced?" and "How do you feel about your teacher, counselor, or doctor?" are personal and may offend some people who might then refuse to give the true answers. When personal information is essential to the survey, you can ask questions in the least emotionally charged way if you provide categories of responses.

Example: Item-Writing Skills—Very Personal Questions

Poor: What was your annual income last year?
          $_____

Better: In which category does your annual income last
          year fit best?
                   Below $10,000
                   Between $10,000 and $20,000
                   Between $20,001 and $40,000
                   Between $40,001 and $75,000
                   Over $75,001

Categories of responses are generally preferred
for very sensitive questions because they do not
specifically identify the respondent and appear less
personal.

7. Each Question Should Have Just One Thought.
Do not use questions in which a respondent's truthful answer could be both yes and no at the same time
or agree and disagree at the same time.

**Example: Item-Writing Skills—One Thought
         per Question**

Poor: Should the United States cut its military or domestic
          spending?
                   Yes
                   No
                   Don't know

Better: Should the United States substantially reduce its
          military spending?
                   Yes
                   No
                   Don't know
   or
          Should the United States allocate more money to
          domestic programs?
                   Yes
                   No
                   Don't know
   or
          If the United States reduced its military spending,
          should it use the funds for domestic programs?
                   Yes
                   No
                   Don't know

TYPES OF RESPONSES FOR SURVEY ITEMS WITH FORCED CHOICES

Yes and No

The responses in a survey with forced-choice
questions can take several forms.

Example: Yes and No Responses

Have you graduated from college?
        Yes
        No
Does your car have four-wheel drive?
        Yes
        No
        Don't know

Yes and no responses are simple to use and score.
But a slight misinterpretation means that the answer
will be exactly opposite from what the respondent
really means. Also, in some cases, asking for absolutely negative or positive views may result in the
participant's refusal to answer.

Checklist

A checklist provides respondents with a series of
answers. They may choose just one or more answers
depending on the instructions.

**Example: Checklist Responses in Which Respondent
         Must Choose**

(One answer only)
Which of the following medicines do you prefer most for
treating a headache?

	Circle one
I don't take medicine for headaches	1
Aspirin	2
Tylenol	3
Anacin	4
Excedrin	5
Other, specify _____	6

Example: Checklist Responses That Respondents Can Check

(Several answers)

Check which of the following medicines you have taken during the past month.

Please give an answer for each medicine.

	1. Took This	2. Did Not Take This
Aspirin	_____	_____
Codeine	_____	_____
Penicillin	_____	_____
Morphine	_____	_____
Corticosteroids	_____	_____
Antihistamine	_____	_____

Checklists help remind respondents of some things they might have forgotten. If you simply asked people to list their medications, chances are some would forget what they have taken. Also, checklists provide the spelling for difficult words. A problem with them is that the respondent might think a choice is familiar when it is not. Did they take penicillin or ampicillin? Was it this month or last? Also, it is somewhat difficult to format and interpret responses to checklists where multiple answers can be given. Suppose in the second example that a person checks aspirin and codeine, but fails to indicate whether or not the other medicines were taken. Can you assume that the others were not taken, or is it possible that they were, but the person did not bother to complete the item?

The Rating Scale

With rating scales, the respondent places the item being rated at some point along a continuum or in any one of an ordered series of categories. A numerical value is assigned to the point or category. There are four types of rating or measurement scales.

1. *Nominal.* These are sometimes called categorical response scales and refer to answers given by people about the groups to which they belong: gender, religious affiliation, school, or college last attended.

Example: Nominal Rating Scale

What is the newborn's gender?

	Circle one
Male	1
Female	2

2. *Ordinal.* These scales require that respondents place answers in rank order. A person's economic status (high, medium, or low) would provide an ordinal measurement. A measure of whether an individual strongly agreed with a statement, agreed, disagreed, or strongly disagreed is considered an ordinal measure by some people and an interval measure by others.

Example: Ordinal Rating Scale

What is the highest level of education that you achieved?

	Circle one
Elementary school	1
Some high school	2
High school graduate	3
Some college	4
College graduate	5
Postgraduate	6

3. *Interval.* With these measurement scales, distances between numbers have a real meaning. Annual income, for example, may be placed in intervals. The $10,000 difference between $20,000 and $30,000 a year means the same as the difference between $50,000 and $60,000 a year. However, having an income of $20,000 does not automatically mean that you are twice as rich as the person whose income is $10,000. Too many variables intervene, such as the number of people in the family, eligibility for assistance, savings, home ownership, and so on, so be careful and consider ratio measurements.

Example: Interval Rating Scale

How many millions of dollars would you be willing to spend on a three-bedroom, two-bathroom house on one-half acre with a pool in Beverly Hills Estates?

1. $1,000,000 to $1,500,000
2. $1,500,001 to $2,000,000
3. $2,000,001 to $2,500,000
4. Money is no object

4. *Ratio*. Height and weight are ratio scales. If you weigh 120 pounds and I weigh 240 pounds, I am twice as heavy as you. A ratio scale, like an interval scale, is one in which adjoining units on the scale are always equidistant from each other, no matter where they are on the scale. In addition, the ratio scale has a true zero. A ruler represents a ratio scale: The inch difference between seven inches and eight inches is the same as the difference between nine inches and ten inches, and zero means the absence of length. With the ratio scale you can say that six inches is twice as long as three inches.

Surveys rarely have ratio measures. Usually, only ordinal or interval scales are available. For simplicity's sake, call interval and ratio scales *numerical*.

Example: Ratio Scale

How many pounds did you weigh on your last checkup?

Weight in pounds:

The distinctions between nominal, ordinal, and numerical scales have more than academic interest. They determine the kinds of statistical treatments you can use. For example, the appropriate measure of "central tendency" for use with a nominal scale is the mode, whereas the medium may be used with an ordinal scale and the mean with a numerical scale (see Chapter 6).

Graphic Scales

For a survey opinion on the city council's effectiveness in resolving certain issues, a graphic scale could resemble that shown in the following example.

Example: Graphic Rating Scale for Assessing a City Council's Effectiveness

Directions:

Make an X on the line that shows your opinion about the city council's effectiveness in resolving the following three issues:

	Very Effective	In Between		Very Ineffective	
Cleaning the environment	1	3	5	7	9
New public transportation	1	3	5	7	9
Hiring new teachers	1	3	5	7	9

Graphic scales are a kind of rating scale in which the continuum of responses is visual. Because of this, you do not have to name all the points on the scale. In this example, only three points are identified: very effective, in between, and very ineffective.

Graphic scales are relatively easy to use. Be careful to put the description as close as possible to the points they represent. If you use the same scale twice for different parts of the questionnaire, be sure it has the same distances between points.

Example: Poor Formatting of Graphic Scales

If you use this scale, stay with it.

Very Effective			Very Ineffective	
1	3	5	7	9

Do not also use this scale in the same survey or question.

A major disadvantage of graphic scales is that they are sometimes hard to interpret. Look at how these three respondents marked the same graphic scale:

Example: Interpreting Graphic Scales

	Agree	Neutral	Disagree

Respondent A

1   2̸   3

Respondent B

1 ✗ 2   3

Respondent C

1   2 ✗ 3

Respondent A has clearly selected a neutral rating. But what about Respondents B and C? Both appear somewhat neutral, with B agreeing more than A and C, and C disagreeing more than either. You can decide to assign all ratings to the nearest point, in this case 2, or you can assume a true continuum, and assign Respondent B a rating of 1.75 and Respondent C a rating of 2.20. Because all graphic scales share this problem in interpretation, the surveyor will always have to decide on a strategy for making sense of the respondents' ratings.

Comparative Rating Scales

Comparative rating scales rely on relative judgments. The most common is the rank order, which is a type of ordinal scale.

Example: Rank Order Scale

Please rank the following five individuals according to their writing ability. The top ranked should be assigned the number 1 and the lowest ranked the number 5.

_____ Fay Gross
_____ Betty Bass
_____ Edward Romney
_____ Alexander Rulman
_____ Marvin Jackson

Another type of comparative scale enables you to contrast a single, specific object in terms of a general situation.

Example: Comparative Rating Scale

Please compare the Imperial Thai Restaurant to others in Los Angeles.

Check one

☐ It is better than most.
☐ It is about the same as most.
☐ It is not as good as most.

To ensure that comparative rating scales provide accurate information, you have to be certain that the respondents are in a position to make comparisons. Do they have experience in judging writing skills? Are they fully acquainted with restaurants in Los Angeles?

Category Scales

When raters use category scales, they select one of a limited number of categories that are previously ordered with respect to their position on some scale:

Example: Category Scales

Frequently
Sometimes
Almost never

Very favorable
Favorable
Neither favorable nor unfavorable
Unfavorable
Very unfavorable

Strongly approve
Approve
Neither approve nor disapprove
Disapprove
Strongly disapprove

Definitely agree
Probably agree
Neither agree nor disagree
Probably don't agree
Definitely don't agree

Are category scales ordinal or interval? Technically, they are ordinal; for many survey purposes, they are used as intervals. In any case, they are easy to use and interpret. How many categories should there be? Some people use as many as nine categories and others as few as three (two is yes or no). An even number of choices, say, four, forces the respondent away from the middle ground ("neither agree nor disagree"). But the needs of the survey and skills of the respondent must determine the number of categories. If very precise information is needed, the respondents are willing and able to give it, and you have the resources to collect it, use many categories; otherwise, use fewer.

Consider these two situations:

Example: Selecting the Number of Categories

1. A four-minute telephone interview was conducted to find out how often families with working mothers ate dinner in restaurants. The question was asked: "In a typical month, how often does your family eat dinner in a restaurant?" The response choices were "two or more times a week," "once a week," and "less than once a week."

2. Physicians were asked to rate the appropriateness of a comprehensive list of reasons for performing selected surgical procedures such as coronary artery bypass graft surgery and gallbladder removal. An appropriate reason was defined as one for which benefits to patients outweighed risks. A scale of 1 to 9 was used, where 1 = definitely inappropriate and 9 = definitely appropriate.

In situation 1, the four-minute interview dictated short responses. In situation 2, physicians were asked to use their expertise to give fairly refined ratings.

ADDITIVE SCALES

Most surveys are designed so that each individual item counts. In a survey of people's attitudes toward living in a trailer park, you might ask 12 questions, each of which is designed in itself to be used to analyze attitudes and therefore is scored separately. Suppose you collected information like this:

- Length of time living in this trailer park
- Ever lived in one before
- Satisfaction with trailer's accommodations
- Satisfaction with park's accommodations
- Satisfaction with quality of lifestyle
- Amenities in trailer
- Age of trailer
- Age of car
- Type of car
- Age of respondent
- Gender of respondent
- Annual income

With this information, you could report on each fact individually or you could look for relationships:

- Between age of respondent and satisfaction with quality of lifestyle
- Between gender and length of time living in the trailer park

Other surveys are different, however, in that the items do not count individually; they must be combined to get a score.

Consider this:

Example: A Survey With an Additive Scale

Doctors at University Medical Center observed that many of their very ill patients appeared to function quite well in society. Despite their disabilities, they had friends and went to the movies, shopping, and so on. Other patients with similar problems remained at home, isolated from friends and family. The doctors hypothesized that the difference between the two groups of patients was in their psychological functioning and access to the resources that make life a little easier for everyone. As part of testing their hypothesis, they plan to give the two groups the Functional Status Inventory developed jointly by the Herbert Medical School and California University. After five years of study and validation, researchers at the two universities have prepared a survey on functioning for use with chronically ill patients. High scores mean good functioning; low scores mean poor functioning.

The methods used to produce an additive scale require sophisticated survey construction skills because you have to prove conclusively that high scorers are in actuality different from low scorers with respect to each and every item. When you use a survey that produces a single score, check to see if evidence is given that it means something.

Defining Additive Scales

Surveyors use the term *scale* in at least two ways. The first refers to the way the responses are organized:

1. Do you eat six or more servings of fruits or vegetables each day?

The response scale is:

Yes	1
No	2

2. How satisfied are you with the examples in this book?

The response scale is:

Very satisfied	1
Somewhat satisfied	2
Somewhat dissatisfied	3
Very dissatisfied	4

The term *scale* also refers to one question or a collection of questions whose scores are meaningful. You have a quality-of-life scale when a survey with ten questions can be scored so that a score of 1 means low quality and a score of 10 means high quality.

Example: A Survey of Foreign Language Skills

Circle the category that best describes your ability to speak each of the following languages.

	Fluent	*Somewhat Fluent*	*Not Fluent*
French	2	1	0
German	2	1	0
Italian	2	1	0
Spanish	2	1	0
Swedish	2	1	0

For each item—French, German, and so on—an ordinal rating scale is used to organize responses. At the same time, by adding all five items together, a scale of language ability can be derived. A respondent who is fluent in all languages would be at one end of the scale, whereas one who is not fluent in any would be at the other. Suppose you assigned 2 points for each language marked "fluent," 1 point each for those marked "somewhat fluent," and no points for "not fluent." A person fluent in all five languages could get a maximum score of 10 points, and someone who was fluent in none would be assigned the minimum score of zero. In this book, this type of scale is called *additive* (because individual responses to items are combined). Among the most commonly used additive scales are the differential, summated, and cumulative.

Differential Scales

Differential scales distinguish among people in terms of whether they agree or disagree with experts. To create a differential scale for an idea such as equality of opportunity, for example, means assembling many statements (e.g., "qualified men and women should receive equal pay for equal work") and having experts rate each statement according to whether it was favorable to the idea. You next compute the experts' average or median ratings for each statement. Then you ask respondents to agree or disagree with each statement. Their score is based on just those items the respondent agrees with. To get it, look at the experts' average score for each statement chosen by the respondent, add the experts' averages, and compute the arithmetic mean to get the respondent's score.

Typically, the directions to users of differential scales go something like this:

- Please check each statement with which you agree.

or

- Please check the items that are closest to your position.

Scoring a differential scale might take this form:

Example: Scoring a Differential Scale

Student A was administered the Physical Fitness Inventory and asked to select the two or three items with which she most closely agreed. These are the two items she chose and the judges' scores.

	Median Scores Assigned by Judges
1. Physical fitness is an idea whose time has come.	3.2
2. Regular exercise such as walking or bicycling is probably necessary for everyone.	4.0

Student A's score was 3.6 (the average of 3.2 and 4.0), which was considered to be supportive of physical fitness. (The best possible score was 1.0 and the worst was 11.0.)

Are there disadvantages to differential scales? Perhaps the most obvious one is in the amount of work needed to construct them. Also, you must take into account the attitudes and values of the judges whose ratings are used to anchor the scale and interpret the responses. The judges may be quite different from the people who might use the scale.

Summated Scales

A summated scale aligns people according to how their responses add up. Suppose a self-esteem questionnaire has a series of items that use the same rating scale (agree, neutral, disagree):

Example: Creating a Summated Scale for a Self-Esteem Survey

Directions: Check if you agree or disagree with each of the following statements.

Check one for each statement.

Statement	Agree	Neither Agree nor Disagree	Disagree
a. At times, I think I am no good at all.	____	____	____
b. On the whole, I am satisfied with myself.	____	____	____
c. I often feel very lonely.	____	____	____
d. My social life is very complete.	____	____	____
e. My friends admire my honesty.	____	____	____

How would you compute a summative scale for this questionnaire? First, decide which items are favorable (in this case, b, d, and e) and which are not (a and c). Next, assign a numerical weight to each response category. You might do something like this:

Favorable = +1 point

Neutral = 0 points

Unfavorable = –1 point

A person's score would be the algebraic sum of his or her responses to five items. The answers Person X gave are shown in the example on the following page.

Example: Scoring a Summated Scale

	Person X's Response			Is Item Favorable (+) or Unfavorable (-)?	Item Score
Statement	Disagree	Neither Agree nor Disagree	Agree		
a. At times I think I am no good at all.	✓			–	+1
b. On the whole, I am satisfied with myself.		✓		+	0
c. I often feel very lonely.			✓	–	–1
d. My social life is very complete.			✓	+	+1
e. My friends admire my honesty.		✓		+	0

Person X disagreed with Item a, which is fundamentally unfavorable, and got a score of +1. For Item b, the person was neutral and so earned a score of 0. Item c produced agreement, but it was fundamentally unfavorable; Person X got a score of –1. There was agreement with Item d, resulting in a score of +1 and a neutral response to e, producing a score of 0. Person X's summated scale score was +1 out of a possible total of +5. (A perfect score of +5 would have come about if Person X answered: a = disagree; b = agree; c = disagree; d and e = agree.)

Likert type scales (such as strongly agree, agree, neither agree nor disagree, disagree, strongly disagree) are summative.

Cumulative Scales

With cumulative scales, people respond to a series of items by indicating the extent of their agreement or disagreement. How are cumulative scales different from others? In cumulative scales, the items are arranged so that an individual who replies favorably to Item 2 also, by necessity, gives a favorable answer to Item 1; one who responds favorably to Item 3 also does so to Items 1 and 2. A person's score is computed by counting the number of items answered favorably and placing him or her on the continuum that goes from favorable to unfavorable that the items, taken together, represent.

Here's how such a scale might work:

Example: Cumulative Scale

Check which of the following jobs young people should be encouraged to pursue. Stop if you answer no to any item.

	Pursue?	
Job	Yes	No
Nurse		
Programmer		
President of the United States		

Interpretation:

A person with a score of 3 would encourage young people to seek all three jobs; a person with a score of 2 would stop at programmer; a person with a score of 1 would accept only nurse from this list.

Cumulative scales are also called Guttman scales. In actual practice, it is always difficult to produce a set of items that constitutes a true Guttman scale, and you need statistical expertise to create one. If you plan to use a Guttman type scale, check to see that it is technically sound. A good rule of thumb is that no more than 10% of the responses should violate the Guttman pattern in which a favorable answer to any given item means favorable answers to all the items that went before it.

Is Additive Scaling Just for the Experts?

The answer is probably yes. It is very difficult to define and measure general attitudes, feelings, and ideas because there are many conflicting theories of personality and development. Lack of agreement prohibits all but the most skillful from attempting to translate the theories into the survey instruments with scaled scores. And even with skill, the costs of scientifically validating additive scales would be beyond many budgets.

The good news is that most surveys do not need to be scaled because your concern will be with each item. Look at these:

- A survey of medical educators is conducted to find out what courses in geriatrics should be required of nursing students.
- Club members are surveyed to find out the goals they believe the organization should pursue.
- College graduates are surveyed to find out the annual salaries they earn from their first full-time jobs.

In none of these surveys would single scores combining all items into an additive scale make sense. Knowledge of scaling principles, however, is probably important. You should also pay careful attention to the scales of surveys you may want to adapt for your own purposes.

3

GETTING IT TOGETHER
Some Practical Concerns

OVERVIEW

How long should a survey be? A survey's length depends on what you need to know, when you need to know it, the amount of time respondents are willing to spend answering questions, and your resources.

The first question on the survey should be clearly connected to its purpose; objective questions come before subjective ones; move from the most familiar to the least and follow the natural sequence of time; keep questions independent to avoid bias; put relatively easy questions at the end (particularly of long surveys), but put "sensitive" questions in the middle; avoid many items that look alike; and place questions logically.

To boost the response rates for self-administered questionnaires, plan in advance and monitor results. Consider sending respondents a letter before the survey begins and also at the time of the survey, offer to send results, keep questionnaires short, and think about offering incentives. Interviews also require preparation and planning. Interviewers should fit in with respondents and need systematic, intensive training. Set up a system for monitoring the quality of the interviews over time.

You should pilot test your survey to see that it can be administered easily and according to plan. Your main goal is reliable and valid survey data. Reliability refers to the consistency of the information you get (people's answers do not keep changing), and validity refers to the accuracy of the information. (A measuring tape would be reliable if it says yesterday and today that you are 2 feet 3 inches tall. This measurement would, however, be invalid if you are actually 5 feet 4 inches tall.)

One way to ensure the reliability and validity of your survey is to base your survey on one that someone else has developed and tested. Check the results, and ask if the survey has proven its reliability. Also, if the survey has more than one form, ask for evidence that the forms are equivalent. Finally, you may want to check if the survey is internally consistent.

When using someone else's survey, check the validity. Predictive validity is a measure of the survey's ability to forecast performance; concurrent validity means the survey and some other measure agree; content validity refers to the accuracy with which the questions represent the characteristics they are supposed to survey. Construct validity is experimentally obtained proof that a survey that is intended to measure a specific feeling, attitude, belief, or behavior truly measures it.

A pilot test helps you design a reliable survey. When pilot testing, anticipate the actual circumstances in which the survey will be conducted, and make plans to handle them. Choose respondents similar to the ones who will eventually complete the survey, and enlist as many people as you can. For reliability, focus on the clarity of the questions and the general format of the survey.

Pilot testing bolsters reliability and validity because it can help you see that all topics are included and that sufficient variety in the responses is available—if people truly differ, your survey will pick up those differences.

The use of surveys and concern for ethical issues are completely interwoven. Surveys are conducted because of the need to know; ethical considerations protect the individual's right to privacy.

The federal government has specified the legal dimensions of informed consent, privacy, and confidentiality. If you do a survey that is supported by federal funds, you may have to obtain clearance, which means proving the necessity and value of your survey to the Office of Management and Budget. Most public and private agencies that conduct surveys, research, and evaluation or perform educational services have policies on informed consent and confidentiality. Be prepared to explain the risks and benefits to respondents if they complete the survey.

LENGTH

The length of a survey depends on what you need to know and how many questions are necessary so that the resulting answers are credible. Another consideration is the respondents. How much time do they have available, and will they pay attention to the survey? Relatively young children, for example, may stay put only for a few minutes. You must consider your resources. A 10-minute telephone or face-to-face interview will cost less than an interview lasting 20 minutes. Here are two situations illustrating how the circumstances under which a survey is conducted influence its length.

Example: How a Survey's Circumstances Can Influence Its Length

Situation 1:   The local library is concerned that it continue to meet the needs of a changing community. In recent years, many more of its patrons are over 65 years of age, and a substantial percentage speak English as a second language. Among the library's concerns are the adequacy and relevance of its exhibits, newspapers, magazines, and other periodicals; programs featuring new books and writers; and special interest collections concerned with such issues as health. A bilingual volunteer will be devoting two mornings and one afternoon a week for eight weeks to a 45-minute face-to-face interview with users of the library. A 50-item survey form has been designed for the purpose.

Situation 2:   The neighborhood library is also concerned that its services are appropriate for a population that is increasingly older and non-English speaking. The city has decided that the neighborhood library is not the only library in the city that is changing in its needs and has agreed to sponsor a survey of its library patrons. To minimize the amount of time that librarians and patrons will have to spend on the survey, a ten-minute, six-item, self-administered questionnaire is prepared by the central library office. Four questions ask about the adequacy of the library's collection of books and magazines, computer access, and special interest collections; two questions ask about the respondent's educational background and income. To facilitate the survey's efficiency, questionnaires are left at the check-out desk, completed at the library, and left with the local branch librarian, who then sends it to the central office for analysis.

PUTTING QUESTIONS IN ORDER

All surveys should be preceded by an introduction, and the first set of questions should be related to the topic described in it. Look at this introduction and first question for a telephone interview.

Example: An Introduction to a Telephone Survey and Its First Question

Hello. I am calling from California University. We are surveying people who live in student housing to find out whether it is a satisfactory place to live. Your name was selected at random from the housing registry, a directory of students who have voluntarily listed their telephone numbers. Our questionnaire will take no more than four minutes. You can interrupt me at any time. May I ask you the questions?

[*If yes, continue. If no, say "Thank you" and hang up.*]

[*Continue here*]

The first question asks you about your overall satisfaction with your apartment. Do you consider it [*Read choices*]:

1. Definitely satisfactory
2. Probably satisfactory
3. Probably not satisfactory
4. Definitely not satisfactory
5. [DO NOT SAY] no opinion, or don't know/wrong answer

The interviewer starts off by saying that questions will be asked about satisfaction with student housing, and the first question calls for a rating of satisfaction. People sometimes respond best when the first questions ask for objective facts. Once they become used to the survey and more certain of its purposes, they are more likely to provide the answers to relatively subjective questions. Suppose you wanted to know about the success of a summer city clean-up program, for example. You might first begin by asking participants how they first heard about the program and how long they had been in it (two questions of fact), and then ask how well they liked their job.

Questions should proceed from the most familiar to the least. In a survey of needs for health services, items can first be asked about the respondent's own needs for services, then the community's, the state's, and so on.

Questions of recall should also be organized according to their natural sequence. Do not ask very general questions: "When did you first become interested in jogging?" or "Why did you choose jogging over other physical exercise?" Instead, prompt the respondent and ask: "When you were in high school, did you have any interest in jogging? When you were in college?"

Sometimes the answer to one question will affect the content of another. When this happens, the value of the questionnaire is seriously diminished. Look at this:

Example: Ordering Survey Questions

Which question should come first?

    A. How much help does your adviser give you?

or

    B. Which improvements do you want in your education?

Answer: Question B should come before Question A. If it does not, then adviser-student relations might be emphasized unduly simply because they had been mentioned.

How about this:

Example: Ordering Survey Questions

Which question should come first?

    A. How satisfied are you with the president's economic policy?

or

    B. What is the quality of the president's leadership?

Answer: Question B should precede A because a person who is dissatisfied with the president's economic policy (and perhaps nothing else) might rate the quality of the president's leadership lower than otherwise.

Place relatively easy-to-answer questions at the end. When questionnaires are long or difficult, respondents may get tired and answer the last questions carelessly or not answer them at all. You can place demographic questions (age, income, gender, and other background characteristics) at the end because these can be answered quickly.

Avoid many items that look alike. Twenty items, all of which ask the respondent to agree or disagree with statements, may lead to fatigue or boredom, and the respondent may give up. To minimize loss of interest, group questions and provide transitions that describe the format or topic:

Example: Providing Transitions

The next ten questions will ask if you agree or disagree with different planks of the Democratic Party platform.

Questions that are relatively sensitive should be placed toward the end. Topics such as grooming habits, religious views, and positions on controversial subjects such as abortion and gun control must be placed far enough along so there is reason to believe the respondent is willing to pay attention, but not so far that he or she is too fatigued to answer properly.

Finally, questions should appear in logical order. Do not switch from one topic to another unless you provide a transitional statement to help the respondent make sense of the order.

Here is a checklist of points to consider in selecting the order for the questions in your survey:

Checklist to Guide Question Order

✓ For any given topic, ask relatively objective questions before the subjective ones.

✓ Move from the most familiar to the least.

✓ Follow the natural sequence of time.

✓ See to it that all questions are independent.

✓ Relatively easy-to-answer questions should be asked at the end.

✓ Avoid many items that look alike.

✓ Sensitive questions should be placed well after the start of the survey, but also well before its conclusion.

✓ Questions should be in logical order.

QUESTIONNAIRE FORMAT: AESTHETICS AND OTHER CONCERNS

A questionnaire's appearance is vitally important. A self-administered questionnaire that is hard to read can confuse or irritate respondents. The result is loss of data. A poorly designed interview form with inadequate space for recording answers will reduce the efficiency of even the most skilled interviewers.

Here are some dos and don'ts:

Do: Put just one question on a line.
    Leave plenty of space for responses.

Don't: Squeeze several questions together.
    Do not abbreviate questions.

Response Format

The general rule is to leave enough space to make the appropriate marks. Here are several response formats.

Example: Response Formats

A. ___✓___ Yes
    _____ No
    _____ Don't know

B. ①. Yes
    2. No
    3. Don't know

C.   *Code*
    Yes   ①
    No   2
    Don't know 3

If you use the format shown as A, be careful to provide enough space so that this doesn't happen:

Poor:
    ___✓___ 1. Yes
    ___✓___ 2. No
    _____ 3. Don't know

B or C is probably safer.

BRANCHING QUESTIONS, OR THE INFAMOUS "SKIP" PATTERN

What happens when you are concerned with getting answers to questions that you know are appropriate only for part of your group? Suppose you were doing a survey of young people's participation in afterschool activities. You know that one major activity might be sports and another might be music, but you also know that only some participate in either.

If you want to ask about a topic that you know in advance will not be relevant to everyone in the survey, you might design a form such as the one in the following example.

Example: Skip Patterns or Branching Questions

3. Do you participate in sports?
   a. No (GO TO QUESTION 4)
   b. Yes

   IF YES Which sports do you perform?

	Yes	No
Soccer	1	2
Track and field	1	2
Other	1	2

or

Do you participate in sports?

   Yes   (COMPLETE SECTION A)

or

   No   (GO TO SECTION B)

You must be extra careful in using branching questions (or, as they are often called, skip patterns) in written self-administered questionnaires. In fact, some surveyors think that skip patterns are confusing to most people and should not be used in written questionnaires at all. Remember, respondents can skip important questions if they are baffled about where to go next on the survey form. Interviewers must be trained to follow the branches or else they might be unable to administer the survey correctly. Computer-assisted surveys are effective vehicles for branching because you can design the software to guide the respondent. For instance, if the survey instruction is, "If no, go to Question 6," the respondent who answers no will automatically be sent to Question 6.

ADMINISTRATION

Self-Administered Questionnaires

Self-administered questionnaires require much preparation and monitoring to get a reasonable response rate. These questionnaires are given directly to people for completion and, usually, very little assistance is available in case a respondent does not understand a question. A survey questionnaire asking about teachers' availability and needs for in-service training may be placed in their office mailbox, for example, with a week's return requested. Of course, teachers who have difficulty with the form

might discuss the problem among themselves, but no guarantees exist that the solution will be just as correct or incorrect as if the individual acted alone. Mailed questionnaires isolate the respondents most, because no one is usually available to clear up confusion.

Advance preparation, in the form of careful editing and tryouts, will unquestionably help produce a clear, readable self-administered questionnaire. To further ensure that you get what you need, you should review the returns. Are you getting the response rate you expected? Are all questions being answered? Here is a checklist for using self-administered questionnaires that can help you get what you need.

Checklist for Using Self-Administered Questionnaires

✓ Send respondents a preletter telling them the purpose of your survey questionnaire. This should warn people that the survey is coming, explain why the respondents should answer the questions, and tell them about who is being surveyed.

✓ Prepare a short, formal letter to accompany the questionnaire form. If you have already sent a preletter, this one should be very concise. It should again describe the survey aims and participants.

✓ Offer to send respondents a summary of the findings so they can see just how the data are used. (If you promise this, budget for it.)

✓ If you ask questions that may be construed as personal—such as gender, age, or income—explain why the questions are necessary.

✓ Keep the questionnaire procedures simple. Provide stamped, self-addressed envelopes. Keep page folding to a minimum so respondents do not feel they are involved in a complicated activity.

✓ Keep questionnaires as short as you can. Ask only questions you are sure you need and do not crowd them together. Give respondents enough room to write and be sure each question is set apart from the next.

✓ Consider incentives. This may encourage people to respond. Incentive may range from money and stamps to pens and food.

✓ Be prepared to follow up or send reminders. These should be brief and to the point. It often helps to send another copy of the questionnaire. Do not forget to budget money and time for these additional mailings.

Interviews

Finding Interviewers. Interviewers should fit in as well as possible with respondents. They should avoid flamboyant clothes, haircuts, and so on. Sometimes it is a good idea to select interviewers who are similar to respondents. If you want to find out why adolescent girls smoke, for example, you might hire young women to do the questioning.

It is also important that the interviewers be able to speak clearly and understandably. Unusual speech patterns or accents may provoke unnecessarily favorable or unfavorable reactions. The interviewer's way of talking is, of course, an extremely important consideration in the telephone interview. You should be keenly aware of the possibility that the interviewer's attitude toward the survey and respondent will influence the results. If the interviewer does not expect much and sends this message, the response rate will probably suffer. To make sure you are getting the most accurate data possible, you should monitor the interviewers.

Training Interviewers. The key to a good telephone or face-to-face interview is training, which should ensure that all interviewers know what is expected of them and that they ask all the questions in the same way, within the same amount of time.

Whether you are training 2 interviewers or 20, it is important to find a time to meet together. The advantage of meetings is that everyone can develop a standard vocabulary and share problems. If the trainees have to travel to reach you, you may have to think about paying for gasoline or other means of private or public transportation.

Once at the training site, trainees must have enough space to sit and write or perform any other activities you will require of them. If you want them to interview one another as practice for their real task, be sure the room is large enough so that two or more groups can speak without disturbing the others. You may even need several rooms.

If training takes more than an hour and a half, you should provide some form of refreshment. If you cannot afford to do that, at least give trainees time to obtain their own.

Trainees should be taken step by step through their tasks and given an opportunity to ask questions. It is also essential to tell them some of the reasons for their tasks so they can anticipate prob-

lems and be prepared to solve them. The most efficient way to make sure the trainees have all the information they need to perform their job is to prepare a manual. Here you can explain what they are to do and when, where, why, and how they are to do it. A three-ring binder makes it easy to add paper, if necessary. Another option is to put the manual on disk and give each person a disk.

Conducting Interviews. Here are some tips on conducting interviews that should be emphasized in your training sessions:

1. Make a brief introductory statement that will describe who is conducting the interview ("Mary Doe for Armstrong Memorial Medical Center"), tell why the interview is being conducted ("to find out how satisfied you are with our hospitality program"), explain why the respondent is being called ("We're asking a random sample of people who were discharged from the hospital in the past two months"), and indicate whether or not answers will be kept confidential ("Your name will not be used without your written permission").

2. Try to impress the person being interviewed with the importance of the interview and of the answers. People are more likely to cooperate if they appreciate the importance of the subject matter. Do not try to deal with every complaint or criticism, but suggest that all answers will receive equal attention.

3. Flexibility is needed. Although it is important to stay on schedule and ask all the questions, a few people may have trouble hearing and understanding some of the questions. If that happens, slow down and repeat the question.

4. Interview people alone. The presence of another person may be distracting and alter results.

5. Ask questions as they appear in the interview schedule. It is important to ask everyone the same questions in the same way or the results will not be comparable.

6. Interviewers should follow all instructions given at the training session and described on the interview form.

Monitoring Quality. To make sure you are getting the most accurate data possible, you should monitor the quality of the interviews. This might mean something as informal as having interviewers call you once a week or something as formal as having them submit to you a standardized checklist of activities they perform each day. If possible, you may actually want to go with an interviewer (if it is a face-to-face interview) or spend time with telephone interviewers to make sure that what they are doing is appropriate for the survey's purposes. To prevent problems, you might want to take some or all of the following steps:

- Establish a hot line—someone available to answer any questions that might occur immediately, even at the time of an interview.
- Provide written scripts. If interviewers are to introduce themselves or the survey, give them a script or set of topics to cover.
- Make sure you give out extra copies of all supplementary materials. If data collectors are to mail completed interviews back to you, for example, make sure to give them extra forms and envelopes.
- Provide an easy-to-read handout describing the survey.
- Provide a schedule and calendar so that interviewers can keep track of their progress.
- Consider providing the interviewer with visual aids. Visual aids may be extremely important when interviewing people whose ability to speak the language may not be as expert as is necessary to understand the survey. Visual aids are also very useful in clarifying ideas and making sure that everybody is reacting to similar stimuli. For example, suppose you wanted to find out whether or not people perceived that the economy was improving. To ensure that everybody had access to the same set of data on the economy, you might show graphs and tables describing the economy taken from the local newspaper for the past one or two years. Another use of a visual aid might be in a survey of people's ideal expectations for a planned community. You might show several different plans and ask people to describe their reactions to each. The preparation of audiovisual aids for use in an interview is relatively expensive and requires that the interviewers be specially trained in using them.
- Consider the possibility that some people may need to be retrained and make plans to do so.

THE SURVEY IS PUT ON TRIAL

Once your survey has been assembled, you must try it out to see that it can be administered and that you can get accurate data. That means testing the logistics of the survey (the ease with which the interviewers can record responses) as well as the sur-'vey form itself. The purpose of the trial (sometimes called a pretest or pilot test) is to answer these questions:

- Will the survey provide the needed information? Are certain words or questions redundant or misleading?
- Are the questions appropriate for the people who will be surveyed?
- Will information collectors be able to use the survey forms properly? Can they administer, collect, and report information using any written directions or special coding forms?
- Are the procedures standardized? Can everyone collect information in the same way?
- How consistent is the information obtained from the survey?

**Reliability and Validity:
The Quality of Your Survey**

A ruler is considered to be a reliable instrument if it yields the same results every time it is used to measure the same object, assuming the object itself has not changed. A yardstick showing that you are 6 feet 1 inch tall today and six months from today is reliable.

People will change, of course. You may be more tired, angry, and tense today than you were yesterday. People also change because of their experiences or because they learned something new, but meaningful changes are not subject to random fluctuations. A reliable survey will provide a consistent measure of important characteristics despite background fluctuations. It reflects the true score—one that is free from random errors.

A ruler is considered to be a vald instrument if it provides an accurate measure (free from error) of a person's height. But even if the ruler says you are 6 feet 1 inch tall today and six months from now (meaning it is reliable), it may be incorrect. This would occur if the ruler were not calibrated accurately, and you are really 5 feet 6 inches tall.

If you develop a survey that consists of nothing more than asking a hospital administrator how many beds are in a given ward, and you get the same answer on at least two occasions, you would have an instrument that is stable and reliable. But if you claim that the same survey measures the quality of medical care, you have a reliable survey of questionable validity. A valid survey is always a reliable one, but a reliable one is not always valid.

Ensuring Quality: Selecting Ready-to-Use Surveys

One way to make sure that you have a reliable and valid survey is to use one that someone else has prepared and demonstrated to be reliable and valid through careful testing. This is particularly important to remember if you want to survey attitudes, emotions, health status, quality of life, and moral values. These factors, and others like them, are elusive and difficult to measure. To produce a truly satisfactory survey of health, quality of life, and human emotions and preferences thus requires a large-scale and truly scientific experimental study.

Some surveys are available for use, however (possibly at a cost to the surveyor), and should always be considered. To find them you can

1. Contact the major publishers of health and psychological tests, the names of which can be obtained from libraries and the Internet.
2. Review the research literature.

In reviewing a published survey (also, in assessing the quality of a homemade form), you should ask the following questions about three types of reliability: test-retest, equivalence, and internal consistency.

First, does the survey have test-retest reliability? One way to estimate reliability is to see if someone taking the survey answers about the same on more than one occasion. Test-retest reliability is usually computed by administering a survey to the same group on two different occasions and then correlating the scores from one time to the next. A survey is considered reliable if the correlation between results is high; that is, people who have good (or poor) attitudes on the first occasion also have good (or poor) attitudes on the second occasion.

Second, are alternative forms equivalent? If two different forms of a survey are supposed to appraise the same attitude, you should make sure that people will score the same regardless of which one they take. If you want to use Form A of the survey as a premeasure, for example, and Form B as a postmeasure, check the equivalence of the two forms to make sure one is not different from the other.

Equivalence reliability can be computed by giving two or more forms of the same survey to the same group of people on the same day, or by giving different forms of the survey to two or more groups that have been randomly selected. You determine equivalence by comparing the mean score and standard deviations of each form of the survey and by correlating the scores on each form with the scores on the other. If the various forms have almost the same means and standard deviations and they are highly correlated, then they have high equivalence reliability. Equivalence reliability coefficients should be high; look for those that are as close to perfect as possible.

Another measure of reliability is how internally consistent the questions on a survey are in measuring the characteristics, attitudes, or qualities that they are supposed to measure. To test for internal consistency, you calculate a statistic called coefficient alpha (or Cronbach's alpha, named for the person who first reported the statistic). Coefficient alpha describes how well different items complement each other in their measurement of the same quality or dimension.

Many surveyors are not at all concerned with internal consistency because they are not going to be using several items to measure one attitude or characteristic. Instead, they are interested in the responses to each item. Decide if your survey needs to consider internal consistency.

Example: Internal Consistency Counts

A ten-item interview is conducted to find out patients' satisfaction with medical care in hospitals. High scores mean much satisfaction; low scores mean little satisfaction. To what extent do the ten items each measure the same dimension of satisfaction with hospital care?

Example: Internal Consistency Does Not Count

A ten-item interview is conducted with patients as part of a study to find out how hospitals can improve. Eight items ask about potential changes in different services such as the type of food that might be served; the availability of doctors, nurses, or other health professionals; and so on. Two items ask patients for their age. Because this survey is concerned with views on improving eight very different services and with providing data on age and education of respondents, each item is independent of the others.

What is adequate reliability? The criterion depends on the purpose of the survey. To compare groups (e.g., employees at Company A with employees at Company B), reliability coefficients of .50 or above are acceptable. To make decisions about individuals, you need coefficients of .90.

Here are some questions to ask about a published survey's validity:

Does the survey have predictive validity? You can validate a survey by proving that it predicts an individual's ability to perform a given task or behave in a certain way. For example, a medical school entrance examination has predictive validity if it accurately forecasts performance in medical school. One way of establishing predictive validity is to administer the survey to all students who want to enter medical school and compare these scores with their performance in school. If the two sets of scores show a high positive or negative correlation, the survey or instrument has predictive validity.

Does the survey have concurrent validity? You can validate a survey by comparing it against a known and accepted measure. To establish the concurrent validity of a new survey of attitudes toward mathematics, you could administer the new survey and an already established, validated survey to the same group and compare the scores from both instruments. You can also administer just the new survey to the respondents and compare their scores on it to experts' judgment of the respondents' attitudes. A high correlation between the new survey and the criterion measure (the established survey or expert judgment) means concurrent validity. Remember, a concurrent validity study is valuable only if the criterion measure is convincing.

Does the survey have content validity? A survey can be validated by proving that its items or questions accurately represent the characteristics or attitudes that they are intended to measure. A survey of political knowledge has content validity, for example, if it contains a reasonable sample of facts, words, ideas, and theories commonly used when discussing or reading about the political process. Content validity is usually established by referring to theories about personality, emotions, and behavior and by asking experts whether the items are representative samples of the attitudes and traits you want to survey.

Does the survey have construct validity? Surveys can be validated by demonstrating that they measure a construct such as hostility or satisfaction. Con-

struct validity is established experimentally by trying the survey on people whom the experts say do and do not exhibit the behavior associated with the construct. If the people whom the experts judge to have high degrees of hostility or satisfaction also obtain high scores on surveys designed to measure hostility or satisfaction, then the surveys are considered to have construct validity. This form of validity is usually established after years of experimentation and experience.

GUIDELINES FOR PILOT TESTING

Here are some basic rules for a fair trial of a survey.

1. Try to anticipate the actual circumstances in which the survey will be conducted and make plans to handle them. For interviews, this means reproducing the training manual and all forms; for mailed questionnaires, you have to produce any cover letters, return envelopes, and so on. Needless to say, this requires planning and time and can be costly.

2. You can start by trying out selected portions of the survey in a very informal fashion. Just the directions on a self-administered questionnaire might be tested first, for example, or the wording of several questions in an interview might be tested. You may also want to try out the survey process initially by using a different method from the one you eventually intend to use. So if you are planning to hand out questionnaires to conference participants, the trial may involve an interview so that any problems with the questions on the form can be discussed. In the end, you should give the survey logistics and form a fair pretrial.

3. Choose respondents similar to the ones who will eventually complete the survey. They should be approximately the same age, with similar education, and so on.

4. Enlist as many people in the trial as seems reasonable without wasting your resources. Probably fewer people will be needed to test a 5-item questionnaire than a 20-item one. Also, if you see that the survey needs little improvement, stop.

5. For reliability, focus on the clarity of the questions and the general format of the survey. Here is what to look for:

- Failure to answer questions
- Giving several answers to the same question
- Writing comments in the margins

Any one of these is a signal that the questionnaire may be unreliable and needs revision. Are the choices in forced-choice questions mutually exclusive? Have you provided all possible alternatives? Is the questionnaire or interview language clear and unbiased? Do the directions and transitions make sense? Have you chosen the proper order for the questions? Is the questionnaire too long or hard to read? Does the interview take too long? (For instance, you planned for a 10-minute interview, but your pilot version takes 20.)

6. To help bolster validity, you should make sure that all relevant topics have been included in the survey (given your resources). For a survey of political attitudes, have you included all political parties? Controversial issues? What else must be included for your survey to have content validity? If you are not certain, check with other people, including the trial-run respondents. Does the survey have room for the expression of all views? Suppose you were surveying people to find out how religious they are. If you had proof in advance that all are very religious, you would not need a survey. Unless you can show that at least in theory you can distinguish the religious from the nonreligious, no one would believe the results. How do you fix this? In the trials, choose people you know are religious and those you know are not and give them the survey. Do their responses differ?

7. Test your ability to get a range of responses. If people truly differ in their views or feelings, will the survey capture those differences? Suppose your survey was of a suburban neighborhood's attitude toward a proposed new high-rise building development. You should administer the survey to people who are both for and against the building. This will help reveal your own biases in how questions are worded and, for closed-ended questions, might help you identify choices that people who feel strongly one way perceive as missing, but that you might not have thought of.

Consider this:

In a pilot of a survey of children's self-report health behaviors, respondents were asked how often they washed their hands after eating. All six children between eight and ten years of age answered "always" after being given the choices "always," "never," and "I don't know." The choices were changed to "almost always," "usually," and "almost never." With the new categories, the same six children changed their answers to two "almost always" and four "usually."

ETHICS, PRIVACY, AND CONFIDENTIALITY

The use of surveys and concern for ethical issues are completely interwoven. Surveys are conducted because of the need to know; ethical considerations protect the individual's right to privacy or even anonymity.

If your survey is for a public or private agency that is receiving federal funds, you should know that the federal government has specified the legal dimensions of informed consent, privacy, and confidentiality. These dimensions include

- A fair explanation of the procedures to be followed and their purposes
- A description of any risks and benefits
- An offer to answer any inquiries
- An instruction that the person is free to withdraw consent and to discontinue participation without prejudice

Confidentiality is protected by the "Protection of Human Subjects" guidelines of the Code of Federal Regulations. Confidentiality refers to the safeguarding of any information about one person that is known by another. A surveyor who has names and addresses of people, even in coded form, must not use this information to reveal identities. In many surveys, confidentiality is a real concern because complete anonymity is virtually impossible. A code number or even sometimes just a zip code can help lead to the survey respondent's identity.

If your agency receives a contract from the federal government, and you want to survey ten or more people in a ten-month period by means of identical questions, you may have to obtain clearance from the Office of Management and Budget. Getting clearance means describing the data you will collect and justifying the need to collect it. You have to prove the following:

- You will collect the necessary information in a manner that puts the least possible burden on your expected respondents.
- The information you will collect does not duplicate data already accessible from the government agency supporting your grant.
- The information you will collect will be useful.

Clearance from the Office of Management and Budget can take from 60 days to one year and is granted for no longer than three years.

If you work for a private agency, organization, or business, you should check the rules of informed consent and confidentiality. Is there a human subjects protection committee or Institutional Review Board (IRB) whose approval you must get? If you are a student, check to see whether you can ask the questions you are planning. Also, you may be part of a larger project that has already received approval for its activities as long as it conforms to certain standards, among them the informed consent of respondents.

Informed Consent

The consent form gives potential respondents sufficient written information to decide whether to complete a survey. Here is a list of contents to include in an informed consent form.

Contents of an Informed Consent Form

- A title, such as "Consent to Participate in Survey."
- The title of the survey.
- The purpose of the survey.
- Procedures to be followed including where the survey will take place and its durations.
- Potential risks and discomforts. These may include answering questions that are personal or being in a closed room for two hours.
- Potential benefits to respondents and society. These may include new knowledge or better information to develop programs or policies. Sometimes the benefits are not yet really known.
- Payment for participation. Say how much, and if no payment is provided, say so.
- Confidentiality. If the respondent's name is to be kept confidential, describe coding procedures, who will have

access to the surveys, and where the completed surveys will be kept. If information is to be shared with anyone, state with whom. You may be required by law to reveal survey results.
- Participation and withdrawal. Can the participants withdraw at any time? What happens to them if they do? (For example, do they still retain any incentives? Will they still receive the same education, social or health care they came for?)
- Identification of surveyors. Who should be called if questions arise about the survey?

A Far-Reaching World: Surveys, Language, and Culture

Many surveys are translated into different languages. If you plan on translating your survey, do not assume that you can automatically reword each question into the new language. Between the original language and the next language often lies cultural gaps. You may need to reword each survey question.

To avoid confusing people and even insulting them because you misunderstand their language or culture, you should follow a few simple guidelines. These involve enlisting the assistance of people who are fluent in the language (and its dialects) and pilot testing the survey with typical respondents. Follow these guidelines.

Guidelines for Translating Instruments

- Use fluent speakers to do the first translation. If you can, use native speakers. The art of translation is in the subtleties—words and phrases that take years and cultural immersion to learn. If you use fluent speakers, you will minimize the time needed to revise question wording and response choices.
- After the translation is completed, have a second fluent speaker translate the survey back into the original language. Does this back-translated survey match the original version? If not, the two translators should work together to make them match.
- Try the resulting survey on a small group (5-10) of target respondents. If the two translators could not agree on wording, let the group decide.
- Revise the survey.
- Pilot test the survey.
- Produce a final version.

If you want to find out the respondents' backgrounds or their ethnicity, you should probably rely on existing questions rather than creating your own. The following question about ethnicity comes from the U.S. Bureau of the Census. Census surveys are available from the U.S. government electronically and by mail.

Example: Question About Ethnicity

Which of the following best describes you?

(Mark (X) one box)

1	☐	White, not Hispanic
2	☐	Black, not Hispanic
3	☐	Hispanic
4	☐	Asian/Pacific Islander
5	☐	Alaskan Native or Native American, not Hispanic
6	☐	Other
		Specify: _____

SAMPLING

OVERVIEW

Should you survey everyone or just a sample? The answer depends on how quickly you need results, if the credibility of the findings will suffer if someone or some group is left out, and your financial and technical resources.

Sampling can be divided into two categories. A probability sample is selected by an objective method (such as drawing names at random from a hat), and you can also calculate each person's chances of selection. Nonprobability samples are convenient: You select only those respondents who are willing and available to complete the survey.

Random and stratified random sampling are two types of probability samples. Random sampling gives everyone who is eligible to participate in the survey a fair chance of selection. But you may come up against a problem. Suppose you have a group of people you want to survey. With random sampling, just by chance, you may get all men (or all women). If you want a 50-50 split, random sampling may not be the best choice. Random stratified sampling can solve your problem. With this method, you divide the total group into two groups or strata, with men in one group and women in the other. To ensure your even split, you draw an equal number of persons at random from each group. If you plan to use many groups, you will need a larger total sample than if you have just two groups of interest.

You can sample individuals or larger units such as schools, offices, and hospitals. These sampling units contain clusters (of students, employees, nurses, physicians, patients), and so the technique is called cluster sampling. Cluster sampling is done because it is efficient. You can choose the units at random. If you do, you will have to use somewhat complex statistical methods to reconcile a relatively small number of sampling units (such as schools) and their larger number of analytic units (such as classrooms and students).

Nonprobability samples include systematic and convenience samples. In systematic samples, every nth (5th or 500th) unit (individuals, schools, factories) is selected from a list of units. If n is randomly selected, systematic sampling becomes like random sampling. In convenience sampling, you select everyone who is available when you need them *if* they meet the criteria for your survey (right age or reading level, voted in the last election, have lived in the community for at least one year, etc.) and if they are willing to complete all questions. Other nonprobability sampling methods include snowball and quota sampling.

How large should a sample be? Relatively larger samples reduce sampling errors. If you want to evaluate the performance of two (or more) groups, statistical methods may guide you in selecting sample sizes that are large enough to detect differences between the groups—if they occur. Statistical methods may also tell you how large a difference you can observe (and if you will be able to observe them) with the sample size you have.

The response rate consists of the number of completed surveys divided by the number of surveys that should have been completed. Survey more people than you need to guarantee you get your sample size. To improve response rate, know and respect the respondents, train surveyors, monitor the quality of survey administration, keep responses confidential, and provide incentives and rewards when possible and ethical.

SAMPLE SIZE AND RESPONSE RATE: WHO AND HOW MANY?

When you conduct a survey, do you have to include everyone? If you decide to sample, you must ask: How many people should be included? If your company has 1,000 employees and you want to survey just some of them, how do you decide how many people to include? Say you want to compare long- and short-term job satisfaction. Statistical methods can help you decide how many persons should be in each of the groups (short vs. long term) to pick up a difference between groups in satisfaction if one exists. Say you have three months to conduct the survey and think you can survey about 300 of the employees. Statistical methods can help you determine how much of an effect you can detect, given the size of the sample your resources allow you to assemble. Some surveys select arbitrary sample sizes (a 10% or 20% sample). These sample sizes may be fine if you are not using the survey as part of a generalizable research study.

Suppose you wanted to find out if your neighbors will support a community vigilance program in which each household takes responsibility for watching at least one other house when the owners are away. Consider also that you define your community as having 1,000 homes. Do you need to include all households? If you do, will the program be more likely to work than otherwise? Here are some questions you should answer.

1. *How quickly are data needed?* Suppose a recent increase in house burglaries was the motivation for the survey and you wanted to get started immediately. If you waited to survey all 1,000 homes in your neighborhood, you might waste precious time.
2. *What type of survey is planned?* If you are going to use a telephone or mailed survey, your survey may take less time than if you plan to interview people in their homes.
3. *What are your resources?* If they are limited, you have to select a survey method such as telephone interviewing rather than home interviewing. Using telephones is probably more efficient than in-person interviews in large neighborhoods.
4. *How credible will your findings be?* If all 1,000 homes participate, then you will have no problem arguing that your survey is representative of the neighborhood. If only ten homes participate, you probably will prefer to scrap the survey.
5. *How familiar are you with sampling methods?* Sampling methods can be relatively simple or complex. National polls and large research studies use very sophisticated techniques that are dependent on the skills of statisticians and other trained experts. Other methods may be easier to implement, but the resulting sample may be less convincing.

How do you select a sample? Two groups of methods are available: probability sampling and nonprobability sampling.

A probability sample is selected by an objective method (such as a computer program that randomly selects winning lottery numbers). Statistical methods are available to calculate the probability that each person has of being chosen (or winning the lottery). A nonprobability sample includes people who are available and willing to take the survey. The sample selection process is not considered objective because not every eligible person has an equal chance. If you are ill on the day of the survey, you will not be able to participate even if you meet all other requirements.

Consider these two cases:

Example: Probability and Nonprobability Sampling

Case 1. A survey aims to find out how teachers in the Loeb School feel about certain school reforms. All 100 teachers' names are put into a hat, the names are jumbled, and the principal selects 50.

Case 2. A survey is conducted to find out from teachers in the Los Hadassah School District their views on certain school reforms. Ten teachers are chosen to be interviewed from each of the district's six elementary schools, 15 are selected from its four intermediate schools, and 60 are chosen from its one high school. Participating teachers are volunteers who were recommended by their principal. They meet the following criteria: They have been teaching in the district for five or more years, they belong to one of three teachers' associations or unions, and they have participated in at least one meeting during the past year on the district's school reform.

In the first survey, a sample of 50 of 100 teachers is chosen from a hat. This type of sampling is consistent with probability sampling because the selection method is objective and you can use a mathematical formula to calculate the probability of each person's being selected. Also, you can expect that the two groups of teachers will not be systematically different. In each group of 50, you are to like to have similar numbers of people who are generous, smart, and healthy and similar numbers who are miserly, not smart, and unhealthy.

In the second survey example, principals make recommendations, and eligible teachers voluntarily choose to participate. Principals may have their favorites. Teachers who volunteer may systematically differ from those who do not. They may be more enthusiastic about the survey or have more time to complete it, for example. This sampling strategy is not objective. It is a nonprobability sample.

PROBABILITY SAMPLING METHODS

Three of the most commonly used probability sampling methods are

- Simple random sampling
- Stratified random sampling
- Simple random cluster sampling

Simple Random Sampling

A simple random sample is one in which each person has an equal chance of being selected from a population. The population contains everyone of interest.

This is simple random sampling:

Example: Simple Random Sampling

You want to select 100 people from philanthropic foundations to survey them about the types of grants they sponsor. A total of 400 people can provide this information. You place their names in any order. Each name is given a number from 001 to 400. Then, using a table of random numbers (see the appendix), you select the first 100 people whose numbers show up on the table.

Each person in this scenario has an equal opportunity for selection. The population consists of 400 people. Chance alone decides which of them is sampled.

This is not random sampling:

Example: Not Random Sampling

You want to sample 100 people from philanthropic foundations to survey them about the types of grants they sponsor. A total of 400 people can provide this information. You select 25 people in four areas of the country.

Some people in this scenario have no chance of selection: those who do not live in your four chosen geographic areas.

Here is another example of simple random sampling:

Example: Random Sampling

Two hundred nurses, therapists, and social workers employed by a Midwest city signed up for an adult day care seminar. The city had only enough money to pay for 50 participants. The seminar director assigned each candidate a number from 001 to 200, and, using a table of random numbers that he found in a statistics textbook, selected 50 names. He did this by moving down columns of three-digit random numbers and taking the first 50 numbers within the range of 001 to 200.

To facilitate simple random sampling for telephone surveys, some surveyors use a technique called random digit dialing. In one of its variations, called the plus-one approach, a digit is added to the telephone number that is actually selected. If the selected telephone number is 311 459 4231, the number called is 311 459 4232. This technique helps to make up for the fact that in many areas of the country, particularly in urban areas, people do not list their telephone numbers. These people are not fair shakes for selection for telephone surveys.

The advantages of simple random sampling are

- It is the simplest of all probability sampling methods.
- Aids are available to assist you. Most statistics textbooks have easy-to-use tables for drawing a random sample; you can use most statistical applications to draw a random sample.

Table A.1 in the appendix contains a table of random numbers.

A major disadvantage of random sampling is that it cannot be used to divide respondents into subgroups or strata (e.g., 60% male and 40% female). To make sure you have the proportions you need in a sample, you need to stratify.

Stratified Random Sampling

In simple random sampling, you choose a subset of respondents at random from a population. In stratified random sampling, you first subdivide the population into subgroups or strata and select a given number or proportion of respondents from each strata to get a sample.

You can, for example, use stratified random sampling to get an equal representation of males and females. You do this by dividing the entire group into subgroups of males and females and then randomly choosing a given number of respondents from each subgroup. This method of sampling can be more precise than simple random sampling because it homogenizes the groups, but only if you choose the strata properly. That is, do not sample men and women unless you are planning to make comparisons between them. You should plan to make comparisons only if you have some reasons to believe, in advance, that those comparisons might be meaningful. In a survey of voter preference, for example, if you have some evidence that men and women vote differently, then it makes sense to be sure that your survey includes enough males and females to compare them. With random sampling alone you might find that by chance you have a survey sample that consists only of men or only of women.

Here is how stratified random sampling works:

Example: Stratified Random Sampling

The University Health Center is considering the adoption of a new program to help young adults lose weight. Before changing programs, the administration commissioned a survey to find out, among other things, how their new program compared with the current one, and how male and female students of different ages performed. Previous experience had suggested that older students appeared to do better in weight reduction programs. The surveyors therefore planned to get a sample of men and women in two age groups—17 to 22 years and 23 to 28 years—and to compare their performance in each of the programs.

About 310 undergraduates signed up for the health center's regular weight reduction program for the winter seminar. Of the 310, 140 were between 17 and 22 years old, and 62 of these were men. Some 170 students were between 23 and 28 years, and 80 of these were men. The surveyors randomly selected 40 persons from each of the four subgroups (male, female, age 17 to 22, and age 23 to 28) and randomly assigned every other student to the new program. The sample looked like this:

University Health Center's Weight Loss Program

	Age 17-22 Years		Age 23-28 Years		
	Male	Female	Male	Female	Total
Regular program	20	20	20	20	80
New program	20	20	20	20	80
Total	40	40	40	40	160

The advantages of stratified random sampling are that the surveyor can choose a sample that represents the various groups and patterns of characteristics in the desired proportions. The disadvantages of stratified random sampling are that it requires more effort than simple random sampling and it often needs a larger sample size than a random sample to produce statistically meaningful results. Remember, for each stratum or subgroup you must have at least 20-30 persons to make meaningful statistical comparisons.

If you have difficulty selecting a stratified random sample, keep in mind that the same increase in precision obtained with stratification can generally be produced by increasing the sample size of a simple random sample. Increasing sample size may be easier than implementing a stratified random sample.

Simple Random Cluster Sampling

Simple random cluster sampling is used primarily for administrative convenience, not to improve sampling precision. Sometimes random selection of individuals cannot be used. It would, for example, interrupt every hospital ward to choose just a few patients from each ward for a survey. Also, sometimes random selection of individuals can be administratively impossible.

One solution to the problem of using individuals as a sampling unit is to use groups or clusters of respondents. This is the purpose of simple random cluster sampling—to avoid being randomly obtrusive.

In simple random sampling, you randomly select a subset of respondents from all possible individuals who might take part in a survey. Cluster sampling is analogous to random sampling except that groups rather than individuals are assigned randomly. This method presupposes that the population is organized into natural or predefined clusters or groups. Here is how it works:

Example: Simple Random Cluster Sampling

The Community Mental Health Center has 40 separate family counseling groups, each with about 30 participants. The directors noticed a decline in attendance in the past year and decided to try out an experimental program in which each individual would be tested and interviewed separately before beginning therapy. The program was very expensive, and the center's directors could only afford to finance a 150-person program at first.

Randomly selecting individuals from all group members would have created friction and disturbed the integrity of some of the groups. Instead, a simple random cluster sampling plan was used in which five of the 30-member groups—150 people all together—were randomly selected to take part in the ex-

perimental program. Each group was treated as a cluster. At the end of the six months, the progress of the experimental program was compared with that of the traditional one.

The advantages of simple random cluster sampling are that it

- Can be used when selecting individuals randomly is inconvenient or unethical
- Simplifies survey administration

The disadvantage of simple random cluster sampling is that it can require complex statistical methods to reconcile sampling units (the hospital, street, school) and analysis units (patients, homeowners, students).

Although in the example you have 150 people in the survey, you really have just five units (the five groups of 30 persons each) to study. Why can't you study each of the 150 persons individually? When people are in groups—classes, clubs, organizations, neighborhoods—they tend to acquire similar characteristics and views. Studying each individual may be redundant because one person may be very similar to the next. The somewhat good news is that the potential confounding effects of sampling one unit and analyzing another can be handled statistically.

NONPROBABILITY SAMPLING METHODS

Nonprobability samples are usually easier to assemble than probability samples. But gains in ease can be met with losses in generalizability.

Systematic Sampling

In systematic sampling, you pick a number, say, 5, and select every fifth name on a list of names that represents the population. If a list contains 10,000 names and the surveyor wants a sample of 1,000, he or she must select every tenth name for the sample.

Suppose you have a list of 500 names from which you want to select 100 people. You can randomly select a number between 1 and 10. If you chose the number 3, you would begin with the third name on the list and count every fifth name after that. Your sample selection will result in the third name, eighth name, 13th name, and so on until you had 100 names. If you select the "start" number at random, systematic sampling resembles simple random sampling.

There is a danger in systematic sampling. Lists of people are sometimes arranged so that certain patterns can be uncovered, and if you use one of these lists, your sample will be subject to a bias imposed by the pattern. For instance, few people have last names beginning with X, Y, and Z, and they may be underrepresented in a systematic sample.

Here is another example. Suppose you are sampling classrooms to survey students about their attitudes toward school. Say also that the classrooms are arranged in this order:

Floor	1	1a	1b	1c
Floor	2	2a	2b	2c
	.	.	.	.
	.	.	.	.
	.	.	.	.
	.	.	.	.
Floor	N	Na	Nb	Nc

Suppose also that you select every third class starting with 1a. The sample will consist of classrooms 1a, 4a, 7a, and so on, to Na. The survey of attitudes toward school can be biased if each "a" corresponds to a location within the school that faces the lawn and is quiet, and the "b" and "c" classrooms face the sports arena and are noisy.

In considering the use of systematic sampling, carefully examine the list first. If you suspect bias because of the order or placement of sampling units (people, classrooms), use another sampling method.

Convenience Samples

A convenience sample is one that you get because people who are willing to complete the survey are also available when you need them. Say you want opinions on the quality of student health services. You plan to interview 50 students. If you stand near the clinic entrance during the day, you can recruit each person walking in. When you have a complete set of 50 interviews, you have a convenience sample. Here are several sources of bias in this sample:

- Students who are willing to be interviewed may be more concerned with the health service than are those who refuse.

- Students who use the service at the time of your interview may be going for convenience; sicker students may use the service at night.
- Students who talk to you may have a gripe and want to complain.
- Students who talk to you may be the most satisfied and want to brag.
- Students may want to talk but may have no time at the moment; these may be working students. Perhaps working students are different from other students (older?) in their needs and views.

Because of bias, convenience samples are unconvincing unless you prove otherwise. Here's how you might improve the credibility of your convenience sample:

- Ask refusers and participants how concerned they are with their health and compare the responses. You may find no differences, and if so, then your convenience sample's findings are supported.
- Visit the clinic at night to find out if students using the health service then are different from the day students in their health status. You may find no differences. Again your sample is supported.
- Ask students if they have a gripe.
- Ask students about their satisfaction.
- Ask students why they refuse to participate. Is it because they presently do not have the time?

Other Nonprobability Samples

Consider these common situations.

Example: Other Nonprobability Samples

1. A survey of 100 deans of law schools, senior partners in large law firms, and judges is conducted to find out to which lawyers they go to solve their own legal problems. The results are published in *Global News and World Reports* under the title "The World's Best Lawyers."

2. What makes college students liberal or conservative? family background? region of the country in which they were born? current religious practices? educational attainment? income? A survey is conducted of members of the Young Conservative Association and the Young Liberal Society. An assessment of the results reveals the reasons for students' views.

In the first example, the "top" lawyers may provide the services needed by deans, senior law firm partners, and judges. Do the rest of us need the services of the so-called best?

In the second example, students in only two organizations are being surveyed. Can we trust that they represent all students including those who belong to other groups or choose not to join any?

These are standard nonprobability sampling techniques:

- *Systematic samples.* Every *n*th person or unit (school, hospital) is chosen.
- *Convenience samples.* Respondents who are willing and available are selected. The respondents may be individuals or clusters (the nearest ten schools).
- *Snowball samples.* Previously identified members of a group identify other members. For example, you select CEOs and ask them to nominate others.
- *Quota samples.* The group is divided into subgroups in specific proportions (similar to stratified sampling).
- *Focus groups.* Ten to 20 persons are brought together. They are usually consumers. A trained leader surveys their views.
- *Expert panels.* Ten to 20 persons are brought together to provide recommendations on controversial issues in, for example, health, social welfare, and education. Surveys are used as part of the consensus-building process.

FINDING THE SAMPLE

How do you find the sample? Before you look, you must decide who should be included in (and excluded from) the survey. Suppose you wanted to evaluate the effectiveness of COMPULEARN, an Internet-based program to keep employees up to date on how to market products electronically. You decide to survey a sample of users and set these standards:

To be included in the survey, respondents must

- Participate in the program for one or more months
- Be able to use FREENet software
- Be 30 years of age and older
- Read English

These eligibility criteria help you narrow your sample. But they do something else as well: They restrict your findings just to other people who also meet the standards. Here's why. After your survey is complete, you will be able to tell about the effectiveness of COMPULEARN only for persons who have been in the program for one or more months, who can use the specified software, and who are 30 years or older and English speaking. A person who is 29 and meets all other standards is by definition ineligible; your results will not apply to 29-year-olds.

Every time you do a survey, you must decide: Do I want to sample everyone or just people or places with certain characteristics? Usually, the answer is "just people or places with certain characteristics," such as schools with 350 or more students.

How do you get the names or list of persons or places to draw from? Consider this example.

How might you find the names, address, and telephone number of each of the people in these two samples?

1. Plastic surgeons in California
2. Male high school English teachers in the Barton School District

The plastic surgeons' names may be found in directories available from professional societies (e.g., American Board of Plastic Surgery). They may also be obtained by combing telephone books or the Internet. You might be able to identify high school English teachers in Barton through the district's personnel records or its Web page, or by conducting a school-by-school survey.

Getting the list of potential respondents is often a complicated activity. To get the list, you are likely to be required to demonstrate your credibility as a surveyor and prove that you will respect the confidentiality of the responses. Once you have done all that, you then have to make certain the list is up-to-date.

HOW LARGE SHOULD YOUR SAMPLE BE?

Some surveys take place with just one group. A poll of a sample of voters is this type of survey sample. The trick is to select a sample that is representative of all voters who interest you. Other surveys are of two or more groups. For example, a survey comparing the career plans of students in the JOBS program with those students in the CAREER program is this second sample. When comparing students' career plans, you may want representative samples of students in both groups. In addition, you have to think about the number of students that you need in each of the two groups so that if a difference exists between them, you have enough "power" to detect it.

Consider these examples.

---

1. *Survey sampling: One group, no intervention or program:* You draw a sample from a population. You want to make certain the sample looks like the population.

Objective: To survey mountain bicyclists 21 years and younger.

Population: Mountain bicyclists.

Question: How many mountain bicyclists do you need to make sure that your sample is a fair representation of mountain bike riders 21 years and younger?

2. *Survey sampling: Two or more groups and an intervention:* You have two groups. You want to compare them for differences after one of the two has been part of a new activity.

Objective: To evaluate a chess program.

Population: Children who are in an experimental chess program and a control group of children who are not.

Question: How many children have to be in each group to detect a positive difference if one occurs?

When you think about sample size, you must also think about the standard error, a statistic that is used to describe sampling errors. Error exists because when you sample, you select from a larger population and the sample is usually different from the population. This difference is a random result of sampling. You can control it, but probably not eliminate it entirely. If you drew an infinite number of samples, the means would form a distribution that clusters around the true population value. This distribution, which has a bell shape, is the so-called normal distribution. In general, larger samples are more likely to collect around the true population mean and be a more accurate estimation of the population mean.

The Standard Error

Larger samples tend to reduce sampling errors when the samples are randomly selected. The statis-tic used to describe sampling error is called the standard error of the mean. It is the standard deviation of the distribution of sample estimates of means that could be formed if an infinite number of samples of a given size were drawn. Consider this: In a survey of 300 randomly selected respondents, 70% answer yes to the question: Is mountain bicycling one of your favorite sports? The surveyor reports that the sampling error is 9.2 percentage points. If you add 9.2 to 70%, or subtract 9.2 from 70%, you get an interval—called a confidence interval—that ranges between 60.8% and 79.2%. Using standard statistical methods, this means that the surveyor can estimate with 95% confidence that the true proportion of mountain bicyclers who answer yes falls within the interval.

The trick is keeping the confidence interval small. In practice, larger samples usually reduce sampling errors in random samples. But adding to the sample reduces the error a great deal more when the sample is small than when it is large. Also, different sampling methods (such as systematic sampling) may have different error rates from random sampling.

Remember that not all errors come from sampling. Although you want a large enough sample to keep the error low, you do not want sample size pressures to distract you so that other sources of errors blight your survey. Other sources of error include ambiguous eligibility criteria, badly designed and administered surveys, and poor returns.

Statistical Methods: Sampling for Two Groups and an Intervention

Suppose you want to compare two groups. First, divide the population in two (say, at random). Then, use statistical calculations (like the ones below) to find out if each group's sample size is large enough to pick up a difference, if one is present. If the population is large, you may want to select a sample, in this example, at random, and then assign persons to the two groups. If you select a sample at random, you have random sampling. If you assign people to groups at random, you have random assignment. If you select all five schools in a city and randomly assign all students in each of the schools to groups, you have nonrandom cluster sampling and random assignment. If, however, you randomly select five schools in a city, assign three to an experiment and two to a control, and put all students in the experimental schools in the experiment, you then have random cluster sampling and nonrandom assignment.

Use the following checklist to get or evaluate a sample size when you have two groups and an intervention.

Sample Size Calculations for Sampling Two Groups and an Intervention

Assemble and clarify survey objectives and questions
Decide the survey's purposes. Consider these:

Survey 1: Quality of Life
Objective: To determine if younger and older women differ in their quality of life after surgery for breast cancer.

Question: Do younger and older women differ in their quality of life after surgery for breast cancer?

Survey 2: Anxiety in School
Objective: To determine the nature and type of anxiety associated with school.

Question: Do boys and girls differ in their anxieties?
How do younger and older students compare?

Each objective or question contains independent and dependent variables. Independent variables are used to predict or explain the dependent variables. They often consist of the groups (experimental or control, men or women) to which respondents belong or their characteristics (under 50 years old, 51 years of age and older). Take the question "Do boys and girls differ in their anxieties?" The grouping or independent variable is gender.

The dependent variables are the attitudes, attributes, behaviors, and knowledge the survey is measuring. In statistical terms, they are the variables for which estimates are to be made or inferences drawn. In the question, "Do boys and girls differ in their anxieties?" the dependent variable is anxieties.

- Identify subgroups

The subgroups refer to the groups whose survey results must be obtained in sufficient numbers for accurate conclusions. In the two surveys above, the subgroups can be identified by looking at the independent variables. Survey 1's subgroups are older and younger women. Survey 2's are older and younger boys and girls.

- Identify survey type and data collection needs

The dependent variables tell you the content of the survey. For example, Survey 1's specific questions will ask respondents about various aspects of their quality of life. Survey 2's will ask about anxiety. Suppose Survey 1 is a face-to-face interview, and Survey 2 is a self-administered questionnaire.

- Check the survey's resources and schedule

A survey with many subgroups and measures will be more complex and costly than those with few. Consider this:

Subgroups, Measures, Resources, and Schedule

	Subgroup	Type of Survey	Comment
Survey 1: Do younger and older women differ in their quality of life after surgery for breast cancer?	Younger and older women: two subgroups	Face-to-face interview	May need time to hire and train different interviewers for younger and older women
			May have difficulty recruiting sufficient numbers of eligible younger or older women
Survey 2: Do boys and girls differ in their anxieties? How do younger and older students compare?	Boys and girls, younger and older: four subgroups	Self-administered questionnaire	May need time to translate the questionnaire from English into other languages
			Must develop methods to ensure confidentiality of responses

The number of subgroups ranges from two to four. Administering, scoring, and interpreting the survey for one group is difficult enough; with more than one, difficulties mount.

- Calculate sample size

Suppose a survey is concerned with finding out whether a flexible worktime program improves employee satisfaction. Suppose also that one survey objective is to compare the goals and aspirations of employees in the program with other nonparticipating employees. How large should each group of adolescents be? To answer this question, five other questions must be answered:

Five Questions to Ask When Determining Sample Size

1. What is the null hypothesis?

The null hypothesis (H_o) is a statement that no difference exists between the average or mean scores of two groups. For example, one null hypothesis for the survey of employee satisfaction is

> H_o = No difference exists between goals and satisfaction (as measured by average survey scores) between employees participating in the program and nonparticipating employees.

2. What is the desired level of significance (α level) related to the null hypothesis involving the mean in the population (μ_o)?

The level of significance, when chosen before the test is performed, is called the alpha value (denoted by the Greek letter alpha: α). The alpha gives the probability of rejecting the null hypothesis when it is actually true. Tradition keeps the alpha value small—.05, .01, or .001—to avoid rejecting a null hypothesis when it is true (and no difference exists between group means). The p value is the probability that an observed result (or result of a statistical test) is due to chance (rather than to participation in a program). It is calculated after the statistical test. If the p value is less than alpha, then the null is rejected.

When differences are found to exist between two groups, and, in reality, there are no differences, that is called an alpha or Type I error. When no differences are found between groups, although in reality there are differences, that is termed a beta or Type II error.

3. What chance should there be of detecting an actual difference?

Power is the ability to detect a difference of a given size if the difference really exists. It is calculated as $1 - \beta$ (Greek letter beta). It is defined as the probability of rejecting the null hypothesis when it is false or of accepting the alternative hypothesis when it is true. You want high power.

4. What differences between means are important? That is, what is a meaningful $\mu_1 - \mu_2$?

Suppose the survey uses the Goals and Satisfaction Scale (GASS). This hypothetical scale has 50 points. If the scale is valid, you will have access to published scoring rules and data describing what the scores mean. Ask: Are higher scores better? How many points make a practical (educational or clinical) difference? The answers to questions like these will help you decide how much difference you want to detect in your two groups.

5. What is a good estimate of the standard deviation (σ) in the population?

The standard deviation (σ, lowercase Greek letter sigma) is a common measure of dispersion or spread of data about the mean.

If the distribution of values or observations is a bell-shaped or normal distribution, then 68% of the observations will fall between the mean ±1 standard deviation; 95% of the observations, between ±2 standard deviations; and 99% of the observations, between ±3 standard deviations. Look at this:

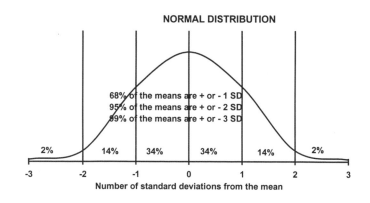

NORMAL DISTRIBUTION

68% of the means are + or - 1 SD
95% of the means are + or - 2 SD
99% of the means are + or - 3 SD

2%   14%   34%   34%   14%   2%

-3   -2   -1   0   1   2   3

Number of standard deviations from the mean

Estimates of the standard deviation can come from previously done surveys. Check that the sample that was used to derive the standard deviation is similar to your own. If it was not, the standard deviation in your group is likely to be different and so is your group.

Another way to estimate the standard deviation in your group is to conduct a small pilot test using about 25 to 50 people. You can also have experts give you estimates on the highest and lowest values or scores as the basis for calculating the standard deviation.

Below is one formula for calculating sample size for comparing the means from two independent groups (such as two groups of employees). Group 1 is in a program to improve satisfaction and Group 2 is not. This formula assumes that the two groups' sample sizes and standard deviations are equal.

$$\frac{(z_\alpha - z_\beta)\,\sigma^2}{\mu_1 - \mu_2}$$

where

$\mu_1 - \mu_2$ is the magnitude of the difference to be detected between the two groups.

z_α (the upper tail in the normal distribution) and z_β (the lower tail) are defined as

$$z_\alpha = \frac{X - \mu_1}{\sigma/\sqrt{n}} \quad \text{and} \quad z_\beta = \frac{X - \mu_2}{\sigma/\sqrt{n}}.$$

Here is an example of how to apply the formula.

Example: Calculating Sample Size in a Survey of Employees in an Experimental and Control Group

Survey Situation. Devsoft's employees are participating in a program to improve their job satisfaction. At the conclusion of the three-year program, participants in the experimental and control groups will be surveyed to find out about their goals and aspirations. The highest possible score on the survey is 100 points. The Type I or alpha level is set at .05. The probability of detecting a true difference is set at .80. A panel of experts in satisfaction measures says that the difference in scores between the experimental and control groups should be 10 points or more. Previous employee surveys found a standard deviation of 15 points.

The Calculations. For the calculation, assume that a standard normal distribution or z distribution is appropriate. The standard normal curve has a mean of 0 and a standard deviation of 1. (For more about the standard normal distribution, one- and two-tailed tests, and z values, see Chapter 6. Actual z values can be found in statistics books.) The two-tailed z value related to $\alpha = .05$ is +1.96. For $\alpha = .01$, the two-tailed z value

is 2.58; for $\alpha = .10$, 1.65; and for $\alpha = .20$, 1.28. The lower one-tailed z value related to β is $-.84$ (the critical value or z score separating the lower 20% of the z distribution from 80%). Applying the formula

$$(1.96 + 0.84)\,(15)^2 = 2\left(\frac{42}{10}\right)^2$$
$$= 2(17.64), \text{ or about } 36$$

at least 36 employees are needed in each group to have an 80% chance of detecting a difference in scores of 10 points.

Sometimes—for practical reasons—you can assemble only a certain number of persons for your survey. How do you know if the number is large enough to find differences? Again, statistics come to the rescue. Look at this:

Example: Power to Detect Differences

The Alcohol Rehabilitation Unit has a program to reduce risks from alcohol use. It sets this standard of success:

> *At the end of the program, 20% of the harmful drinkers in the treatment group will reduce their risks, whereas 10% of the harmful drinkers in the control group will do so.*

The unit hopes to be able to survey 150 persons in each group regarding their risks. Is this sample large enough? A statistician is called in to answer the question. The statistician produces this table for comparing percentage changes using a two-sided test with $\alpha = .05$.

N or Sample Size	%1	%2	Power
50	20	10	.29
100	20	10	.52
150	20	10	.69
200	20	10	.81
250	20	10	.89
300	20	10	.93

You interpret this table as follows:

"If we have 150 persons (final analytic sample size) in the experimental group and 150 in the control group, we will have 69% power to distinguish a shift of 20% in the experimental group from harmful to less risky from a shift of 10% in the control group."

You can use a statistical approach to distinguish different *effect sizes*. The effect size when comparing two means is the difference between them divided by the average standard deviation. Look at this:

Example: 80% Power

The Alcohol Rehabilitation Unit will have complete survey data on 150 persons in an experimental group and 150 in a control group. These persons will have completed a survey before they participate in the unit and immediately after. How much power will this sample size yield? Power is the ability to detect a difference or effect. Put another way, it is the ability of a statistical test to detect an alternative hypothesis of difference (between groups) of a specified size when the alternative is true (and the null is rejected). A statistician provides this table:

N or Sample Size	Effect Size
50	.56
100	.40
150	.32
200	.28
250	.25
300	.23

You interpret this table as follows:

"If we have 150 (final analytic sample size) in our experimental group and 150 in our control group, we will be able to distinguish a .32 effect size between the difference over time in the experimental group versus the difference over time in the control group."

Because you estimate effect by dividing the difference by the standard deviation, you can see, for example, if the experimental group mean improvement was .50 standard deviations and the control group mean improvement in risks was .10 standard deviations, then the effect size would be $50 - 10 = 40 > .32$. In this case, you will have at least 80% power to detect the difference of .40 between the treatment and control groups.

Sample Sizes, Effects, and Power: Statistical Terms. Unless you plan to learn statistics, call in an expert to help. The above discussion is to assist you in learning terminology and to aid you in evaluating the usefulness of your sampling methods and outcomes.

RESPONSE RATE

The response rate is the number of persons who respond (numerator) divided by the number of eligible respondents (denominator). If 100 people are eligible and 75 completed surveys are available for analysis, the response rate is 75%.

All surveys hope for a high response rate. No single rate is considered the standard, however. In some surveys, between 95% and 100% is expected; in others, 70% is adequate.

Here are some tips to improve the response rate:

Tips for Improving Response Rate

- Know your respondents. Make certain the questions are understandable to them, to the point, and not insensitive to their social and cultural values.
- Use trained personnel to recruit respondents and conduct surveys. Set up a quality assurance system for monitoring quality and retraining.
- Identify a larger number of eligible respondents than you need in case you do not get the sample size you need. Be careful to pay attention to the costs.
- Use surveys only when you are fairly certain that respondents are interested in the topic.
- Keep survey responses confidential or anonymous.
- Send reminders to complete mailed surveys, and make repeat phone calls.
- Provide gift or cash incentives.
- Be realistic about the eligibility criteria. Anticipate the proportion of respondents who may not be able to participate because of survey circumstances (such as incorrect addresses) or by chance (they suddenly get ill).
- Formally respect each respondent's privacy.

5

SURVEY DESIGN
Environmental Control

OVERVIEW

A survey's design describes the frequency of administration (twice), when the administration takes place (before and after), and the number of groups to be surveyed.

A cross-sectional design provides a portrait of things as they are at a single point in time. A poll of voters' preferences one month before an election and a survey of the income and age of voters in the same election both use cross-sectional designs.

Longitudinal surveys are used to find out about change. Trend designs are longitudinal. When you survey one group of sixth graders in 1998, another group in 2000, and a third group in 2002, you have a trend design. Another longitudinal design is the cohort. If you take a sample of children who were sixth graders in 1998, and in 1999 take another sample from the 1998 group, you are studying cohorts. A third longitudinal design is the panel. When you take 100 children who are sixth graders in 1998 and survey the same 100 in 2000, you have a panel design.

In comparison group survey designs, the groups you survey can be assembled randomly or in some other way, perhaps voluntarily. Random assignment usually makes it easier to draw valid conclusions from survey data. Normative designs take two forms. In the first, two groups are compared, but only one is actually surveyed; the other group, the comparison, consists of data that are already on record. The second type of normative design uses a "model" as a standard for comparison.

A case control design is one in which groups of individuals are chosen because they have (the case) or do not have (the control) the condition being studied, and the groups are compared with respect to existing or past attitudes, habits, beliefs, or demographic factors that are judged to be of relevance to the causes of the condition.

WHAT DESIGNS ARE AVAILABLE?

Survey data can be used to describe the status of things, show change, and make comparisons. You must choose a design that will result in the kind of data you need. The *design* refers to the way in which the survey environment is controlled or organized. The more control you have, the more credible your results will be. The variables over which surveyors have control are as follows: (1) when the survey is to be given (e.g., after graduation); (2) how often

the survey is to be given (e.g., once a year for three years); and (3) the number of groups (e.g., one, a sample of graduates; or two, all people in Programs A and B).

During sampling, choosing the sample and getting an adequate sample size and response rate are the main issues. When designing a survey, the chief concerns are with when and how often the survey will be given and to how many groups (no matter how the groups were selected or their size).

Look at these five surveys planned by the Have-A-Heart Association.

TABLE 5.1 Relationships Among Purposes, Sampling and Design Concerns, Results, and Type of Design in Five Surveys Given by the Have-A-Heart Association

The Survey Is to Find Out About	Concerns of Sampling	Concerns of Design	Results	Type of Design
Preferences for educational programs	A random sample of program graduates	When conducted: this year	Description of preferences	Cross-sectional
Knowledge acquired from educational programs	Different random samples of graduates	When conducted: 1998, 1999, 2000	Estimate of changes in knowledge	Longitudinal: trend
Attitude toward diet in prevention of heart disease	Samples of randomly selected and possibly different graduates of the original program	When conducted: 1990, 1995, 2000, 2005	Estimate of changes in attitude	Longitudinal: cohort
Attitude toward diet in prevention of heart disease	Same sample of 500 program graduates	When conducted: every five years	Estimate of changes in attitude	Longitudinal: panel
The merits of the program	Randomly selected graduates from Program A and graduates from Program B	When conducted: once when program is completed	How many groups: Two (A and B)	Comparison of knowledge and attitudes

Example: Surveys With Differing Designs

1. The Have-A-Heart Association offers educational programs to people in the community. In June it is conducting a survey of a random sample of people to find out and describe which programs they prefer.
2. The Have-A-Heart Association wants to know how much knowledge people acquired in its educational programs. Surveys have been conducted with random selections of participants from programs that were offered in 1998, 1999, and 2000, and the results were compared.
3. The Have-A-Heart Association has been concerned with monitoring community attitudes toward the role of a proper diet in the prevention of heart disease. An educational campaign was launched in 1990. Every five years since then, the association has been monitoring attitudes by surveying a different random sample of people who were in the original program. This means that some people are surveyed more than once, and others are not surveyed at all.
4. The Have-A-Heart Association has been concerned with monitoring attitudes toward the role of a proper diet in the prevention of heart disease. An educational campaign was launched in 1990. Every five years since then, the association has been monitoring the attitudes of the same 500 people who were in the original program and have volunteered to participate as long as the survey lasts.
5. The Have-A-Heart Association is considering the merits of two competing six-month programs to prevent heart disease. A survey comparing participants' knowledge and attitudes toward diet and exercise will be conducted at the program's completion from random samples of participants in Programs A and B.

The first survey is to be conducted in June to describe the programs that the community prefers. The design, in which data are collected at one point in time, is called cross-sectional.

The second survey calls for collecting information over a three-year period and comparing each year's results with the others. This is called a longitudinal design, and, specifically, a trend design.

The third survey means that every five years you survey a different random sample of people from the original program. This design is called a cohort.

In the fourth survey, the same group provides respondents for a longitudinal study, and the design is called a panel.

The fifth survey is different in that it calls for comparisons between two programs and requires a comparison group design.

Table 5.1 shows the relationship among the purposes, sampling and design concerns, results, and type of design for the five Have-A-Heart Association surveys.

CROSS-SECTIONAL SURVEY DESIGNS

With this design, data are collected at a single point in time. Think of a cross-sectional survey as a snapshot of a group of people or organizations. Suppose the Have-A-Heart Association wants to know which of its educational programs the com-

TABLE 5.2 Educational Programs Preferred Most by Men and Women Participants

	Men		Women		Total	
	No.	*%*	*No.*	*%*	*No.*	*%*
Dine-Out	168	34	175	35	357	69
Feel Fit	75	15	50	10	97	25
Emergency Care	21	4	11	2	46	6
Total	264	53	236	47	500	100

TABLE 5.3 Educational Programs Preferred Most by Participants of Different Ages

	21-45		46-65		66+		Total	
	No.	*%*	*No.*	*%*	*No.*	*%*	*No.*	*%*
Dine-Out	99	20	96	19	41	8	236	47
Feel Fit	35	7	37	7	90	18	162	32
Emergency Care	47	9	52	10	3	1	102	21
Total	181	36	185	36	134	27	500	100

munity prefers. Consider this question and its answer.

Example: Cross-Sectional Design

Question:	If only one program were possible, which would you choose?
Sample:	A cross-section of 500 people, randomly selected, who attended an education program this year
Design:	Cross-sectional
Method:	Telephone interviews
Answer:	Dine-Out wins. The evidence is in Tables 5.2 and 5.3.

Assuming that a sample of participants has been wisely chosen by a random sampling technique and the right questions have been asked, the tables in the example reveal that Dine-Out is the winner. This is why:

1. Regardless of gender or age, Dine-Out is ahead.
2. More men than women prefer Feel Fit and Emergency Care. But when it comes to Dine-Out, men and women have nearly the same preference.
3. People over age 65 prefer Feel Fit, but there are not so many of them as people in the other two categories.

Of course, you might want to use only Table 5.2 or just Table 5.3 to make a point about your survey. You can also combine them into one large table. But a cross-sectional design that is carefully planned will give you a variety of ways for analyzing and presenting your survey data.

With this program preference data, for example, you might also have considered profession—How do people in business and the professions compare? Does retirement make a difference?—or residence—How do people in one part of the city compare with people in some other part?

Cross-sectional surveys have several advantages. First, they describe things as they are so that people can plan. If they are unhappy with the picture a cross-sectional survey reveals, they can change it. Cross-sectional surveys are also relatively easy to do. They are limited, however, in that if things change rapidly, the survey information may become outdated. Also remember that numbers alone may not tell the whole story. Sometimes you have to do statistical tests to find out if differences are meaningful. For instance, if 300 people say yes and 250 say no, is the difference significant?

LONGITUDINAL SURVEYS

With longitudinal survey designs, data are collected over time. At least three variations are particularly useful.

Trend Designs

A trend design means surveying a particular group, for example, sixth graders, over time (e.g., once a year for three years). Of course, the first group of sixth graders will become seventh graders next year, so you are really sampling different groups of children. You are assuming that the information you need about sixth graders will remain relevant over the three-year period. Look at this example with participants in programs sponsored by the Have-A-Heart Association:

Example: Trend Design

Question: What do participants know about heart disease?
Sample: Random samples of 500 participants attending Dine-Out in 1998, 500 in 1999, and 500 in 2000.
Design: Longitudinal, trend
Method: Self-administered questionnaires distributed and supervised by program instructors
Answer: In all three years, participants consistently know little about disease prevention, but by 1999 and 2000, they are beginning to learn about diet, and they appear to know the causes of heart disease by 2000.

Proof is displayed in the following table.

Participants' Knowledge of Heart Disease (N = 1,500)

	Cause of Disease	*Nutrition*	*Prevention*
1998	Little	Little	Little
1999	Some	Some	Little
2000	Much	Some	Little

SOURCE: Scores on the Heart Disease Information Scale, Health Survey Foundation, Los Angeles, 1997.

As with cross-sectional studies, you could have analyzed the results of the heart disease knowledge survey by comparing men and women, different age groups, professions, and so on.

Cohort Designs

In cohort designs, you study a particular group over time, but the people in the group may vary. Suppose, for example, you wanted to study certain people's attitudes toward diet as a means of preventing heart disease after they have participated in a special program sponsored by the Have-A-Heart Association.

You might survey a random sample of the program's participants in 1995, and then, in 2000, choose a second random sample from the 1995 participants and survey them. Although the responses of the second sample might turn out to be entirely different from the first, you would still be describing the attitudes of 1995 participants.

Think about this example, in which surveyors follow participants from a program first given in

1995 to find out about attitudes toward diet and how those attitudes changed over time.

Example: Cohort Design

Question: How have attitudes toward diet changed since 1985?
Sample: A different random sample of participants is surveyed every five years from among the graduates who participated in the Have-A-Heart Association program in 1985.
Design: Longitudinal, cohort
Method: Mailed self-administered questionnaires
Answer: In general, attitudes toward diet have improved dramatically since 1985. No relationship was found between gender and attitude, however.

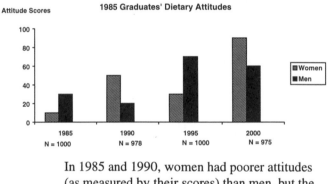

In 1985 and 1990, women had poorer attitudes (as measured by their scores) than men, but the situation was reversed in 1990 and 2000.
For proof, see the figure above.

As can be seen from the figure, men's and women's attitudes fluctuated with time, although they both improved. What happened? Unless you systematically monitor the events that affect the graduates of the 1985 program, you will not be able to tell just by looking at the survey results.

Panel Designs

Panel designs mean collecting data from the same sample over time. If you were concerned with monitoring attitudes toward diet of male and female graduates of an educational program given in 1985, you would select a sample of participants and follow them and only them throughout the desired time period.

One way to display the results of your data might be as shown in the following example:

Example: Panel Design

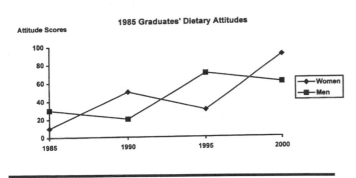

1985 Graduates' Dietary Attitudes

COMPARISON GROUP SURVEY DESIGNS: QUASI- AND TRUE EXPERIMENTS

With these designs, people are divided into two or more groups. The classic comparison group design contrasts an experimental group with a placebo group. Consider this:

A. A survey is conducted of voters' preference for candidates for the school board. As part of the analysis, the preferences of men and women are then compared.

B. How do you get people to participate in school board elections? A month before the elections, two groups of volunteers were assembled. The first group was given a videotaped presentation, and the second was given a talk by prominent people in the community. A survey was taken a week after the election to compare the number of people who voted.

Only B uses a comparison group design because the two groups were specifically created for comparison purposes.

Comparison group designs are sometimes divided into quasi- and true experimental designs. In quasi-experimental designs, assignment to groups is usually deliberate and not at all random. In true experimental designs (also known as randomized controlled), individuals may become members of one group or another; it is mainly a matter of chance. True experiments are the more powerful.

Sometimes longitudinal designs and comparison group designs can be combined. If the various groups included in a comparison group design are each surveyed several times (e.g., every two months or two years), the result is both a longitudinal design and a comparison group design.

Example: A Quasi-Experimental Design

You have been asked to evaluate two programs for elderly persons. Eligible participants are assigned to the programs on a first-come, first-served basis, resulting in 60 people in Program 1 and 59 in Program 2. One of the issues addressed by a survey is whether the participants are satisfied with the staff of their program. To answer this question, you ask participants in both groups to complete a questionnaire at the end of three months' treatment. The design for this survey looks like this:

Attitudes Toward Staff Participants in Two Programs for Elderly Persons

Program 1	Program 2
N = 60	N = 59

DATA SOURCE: Scores on Attitude to Staff Questionnaire.

How valid is the quasi-experimental comparison group design used for the survey of the attitudes of elderly persons in two programs toward their staff? Consider these possibilities:

1. Participants in the two groups may be different from one another at the beginning of the program. For example, older persons may choose one program over the other.

2. Participants who truly dislike the staff in one of the programs may have dropped out of the programs.

Example: A Quasi-Experimental Comparison Group and a Longitudinal Design

Another question posed for the evaluation of the two programs for elderly persons is whether participants have learned about commonly prescribed drugs. To answer this question, participants have been interviewed at three times: at the beginning, at the end of the first month, and at the end of the first year. This survey design strategy can be depicted as follows:

**Changes in Knowledge of Commonly
Prescribed Pharmaceuticals in Two Programs**

Time	Program 1 (N = 60)	Program 2 (N = 59)
Beginning of program		
End of first month		
End of year		

DATA SOURCE: Interview with participants in each program.

The validity of this design may be threatened if persons with serious health problems are by chance more often assigned to one program over the other or by a different drop-out rate.

**Example: A True Experimental Comparison
Group Design**

The government commissioned a survey to determine which of three programs for elderly persons was the most effective. Among the concerns was the cost of the programs. A comparison group design was used in which people at the Freda Smith Center were randomly assigned to one of three programs, and costs of the three programs were compared. Program 1 had 101 people; Program 2, 103; and Program 3, 99.

**Comparison of the Costs of Three Programs
for Elderly Persons at the Freda Smith Center**

Program 1 (N = 101)	Program 2 (N = 103)	Program 3 (N = 99)

DATA SOURCE: Interviews with financial experts.
NOTE: Participants were randomly assigned to programs.

This design is an extremely powerful one. Because people were randomly assigned to each program, any sources of change that might compete with the program's impact would affect all three groups equally. However, remember that although people were assigned randomly to the programs within the Freda Smith Center, other centers may differ, and therefore, the findings from the survey may not be applicable to other places.

**Example: A True Experimental Comparison Group
Design and a Longitudinal Design**

Programs 1 and 2 at the Freda Smith Center proved to be equally cost-effective. The government then commissioned a study to determine which program was considered by participants to deliver the better medical care. To make the determination, a comparison group design was selected in which care was assessed from the beginning and end of the program and compared among people in Programs 1 and 2. The design was depicted by the following diagram.

**Comparison of Medical Care Received by
Participants in Two Programs for Elderly Persons**

Time	Program 1 (N = 101)	Program 2 (N = 103)
Beginning of program		
Completion of program		

DATA SOURCE: ABY Quality of Care Review System; surveys of doctors, nurses, patients.

This true-experiment and longitudinal design is among the most sophisticated and will enable you to make very sound inferences.

OTHER SURVEY DESIGNS: NORMATIVE AND CASE CONTROL

Two lesser-known survey designs are the normative and case control. Both offer some control over the survey's environment by making use of special comparison groups.

Normative Survey Design

Normative designs can take two forms. In the first, two groups are compared, but only one is actually surveyed. The second group, the comparison, is represented by data that are already on record from a previous data collection effort. The second type of normative design appoints a "model" and compares another group to it. Look at these:

Example: Normative Design—Data on Record

The pride of participants in the Los Angeles Youth Program was measured using the PROUD Survey, an instrument that had been validated on a national sample of 5,000 people. The national sample was used as a norm, because there was no reason to believe that the L.A. group would be different in pride than the nation. Youth Program scores were thus compared to the national sample's.

Example: Normative Design—The Model

Are physicians in a new academic medical center as satisfied with their work as are physicians in an older one? The new center has the same mission as the older one. To answer the question, physicians in both centers are surveyed and the new is compared to the older, model center.

Normative data can be based on the activities of other groups or programs. Normative survey designs can be less expensive and time-consuming than are other comparison designs. Remember, your group and the "normal" one may actually differ in important respects, and your survey results will then be less than valid. Suppose the participants in the Youth Program of Los Angeles were younger than the national sample, for example. If age and self-esteem were related, with maturity associated with better survey scores, then the Youth Program would have to work harder to be a success. If you use normative designs, be prepared to defend your choice of norm.

Case Control Design

A case control design is one in which groups of individuals are selected because they have (the case) or do not have (the control) the condition being studied, and the groups are compared with respect to existing or past attitudes, habits, beliefs, or demographic factors that are judged to be of relevance to the causes of the condition.

Case control designs are generally used by researchers who are testing a specific hypothesis, for example, that a connection exists between lung cancer and cigarette smoking habits. Sometimes researchers use case control designs primarily to explore and have no hypothesis. A case control design might be used, for example, in a new study to help find out if certain crucial differences existed between people who are prone to headaches and those who are not.

A case control design needs two groups, and so a major concern is their selection. Ideally, the two groups should be as alike as possible. Their only difference should be that the case has the condition being studied and the control does not. Most often, case control designs mean selecting a control that is like the case in ways that are strongly suspected to affect the condition. In a study of people with headaches, the control might be matched to the case so it had a similar proportion of males, females, and so on.

The major weakness of case control design is that the two survey groups may not be alike at all no matter how selected or matched because of impossibility in controlling for all characteristics that may affect the condition. Some matching criteria might be incorrect, for example, or others may be excluded. Here is how a survey could be used with a case control design.

Example: Case Control Design

The Medical Clinic randomly selected 100 of its 2,500 patients between 21 and 55 years of age who were prone to headaches and 100 who were not. Half the people in each group were male, and half were female. A survey was conducted to find out about the following in relation to each group:

- Typical daily activities
- Potential sources of stress
- Family history and background
- Medical history
- Diet

6

ANALYZING DATA FROM SURVEYS

OVERVIEW

Some methods commonly used to analyze survey data are

1. *Descriptive statistics.* These include counts, proportions, measures of central tendency, and measures of variation.
2. *Correlations.* These show relationships.
3. *Differences.* These include chi-square, *t* tests, and analysis of variance (ANOVA).
4. *Changes.* Special forms of *t* tests and ANOVAs can be used to measure change over time.

The chi-square is used with categorical data. It tests the hypothesis that proportions are equal. The *t* test allows you to compare the average means (averages) of two groups to determine the probability that any differences between them are real and not due to chance. The Mann-Whitney *U* test (also called the Wilcoxon rank sum) enables you to compare two independent groups when you cannot use the *t* test, say, because the sample size is too small. This statistical method tests the equality of the medians. Group means can also be tested with ANOVA, and this method lets you compare several groups. Of necessity, you will need larger samples as you expand the number of comparison groups.

Risks and odds are used to describe the likelihood that a particular outcome will occur within a group, or they can be used to compare groups. When you use risks and odds to compare groups, you compare the *relative* likelihood that an outcome will take place. The relative risk expresses the risk of a particular outcome in the experimental group relative to the risk of the outcome in the control group. The odds ratio is a description of the comparison of the odds of the outcome in the experimental group with the odds in the control group.

Seven questions must be answered before the best method for analyzing data can be determined:

1. How many people are you surveying?
2. Are you looking for relationships or associations?
3. Will you be comparing groups?
4. Will your survey be conducted once or several times?
5. Are the data recorded as numbers and percentages or scores and averages?
6. How many independent and dependent variables interest you?
7. Are the data high quality?

In testing statistical hypotheses, you must establish rules that determine when you will accept or reject a null hypothesis. The null states that the means are equal. A Type I error is the probability of rejecting the null hypothesis when it is true. A Type II error is when you accept a null hypothesis that is incorrect. A confidence interval is a range of values within which the true value such as a mean lies. You can plot confidence intervals on a graph. If the intervals do not overlap, differences exist. If the mean of one group is contained in the interval of the second, differences do not exist. If the intervals overlap, but not the means, you cannot tell.

WHAT IS TYPICAL ANYWAY? SOME COMMONLY USED METHODS FOR ANALYZING SURVEY DATA

The day has arrived. All the surveys have been returned. The response rate is high. All the questions and all the forms have been filled out. Now is the time to find out what the survey shows: How many men responded? women? Do they differ? Have their views changed in the past five years? Surveyors answer questions like these by analyzing survey responses to obtain tallies and averages and to look for relationships, differences, and changes.

Some analysis methods commonly used in surveys are:

1. *Descriptive Statistics.* These are the most commonly used, and they are the basis for more advanced techniques. Descriptive statistics for surveys include counts (numbers or frequencies); proportions (percentages); measures of central tendency (the mean, median, and mode); and measures of variation (range, standard deviation).

2. *Correlations.* These statistics show relationships. A high correlation between height and weight, for example, suggests that taller people weigh more and that heavier people are taller. A Spearman rank-order correlation is used with categorical data, those that come from nominal or ordinal scales. It provides you with a measure the degree of association or equivalence between two sets of ranks as in this example.

Example: Rank-Order Correlation

A class of 50 college students is administered two attitude surveys. The first polls their views on affirmative action, and the second asks about their political preferences. John scores highest among the respondents on one measure, and average on the second; Jane's scores are the fifth and eighth highest; Bill's scores are the 14th and 13th; and so on. A rank-order correlation coefficient is computed to see if the two surveys agree: Do people who rank high on one also rank high on the other?

Pearson product-moment correlations are used to establish relationships between two sets of continuous data such as height and weight. Here are two situations in which these correlations are appropriately used:

- Grade point averages and scores on an attitude toward school survey are correlated.
- Liberal and conservative views (1 = liberal to 10 = conservative) and family income (from \$5,000 to \$50,000) are correlated.

3. *Differences.* Suppose you want to know if one group of respondents is different from another. Are they healthier? More likely to vote in the next election? More employable? Better spellers? Statistical methods used to test for differences in outcomes of surveys include the chi-square test and analysis of variance (ANOVA). Many of these methods actually hypothesize that the survey outcomes are the same across groups! The test of equality—the respondent groups are the same—is called the null hypothesis. Next, the statistical analysis is performed, a statistic is produced, and this serves as a guide in accepting or rejecting the null hypothesis. If the null is rejected in favor of an alternative hypothesis (the groups are different), then the results are considered statistically significant.

Suppose you survey people on a cruise, one half of whom are part of an experimental program combining tourism with education. You are fairly certain that the experiment is working. Nevertheless, you start out with the assumption that both groups are equally satisfied. Then you compare the two groups' average satisfaction scores using a statistical method called an independent *t* test. You find that you are correct and so you reject the hypothesis of no difference. Because the average satisfaction scores of the experimental group were higher, you conclude that the experiment is working, you were right in the first place, and now you have statistics to back you up.

Here are some commonly used techniques for testing for differences among groups, or more precisely, testing whether or not they are the same.

Chi-Square

The chi-square is used with categorical data. It tests the hypothesis that proportions are equal. A proportion is what you get when you find out how many people of all possible people answer a certain way or have a specific characteristic. Suppose you sample 100 people and find that 25 have blue eyes. The proportion of people with blue eyes is 25/100. Suppose that of the 25, 6 are women. If you want to compare the proportion of men and women with blue eyes, chi-square is the right choice. The symbol for chi-square is χ^2.

Example: Chi-Square

The Prison Organization surveys 60 imprisoned men and 40 imprisoned women to find out if they perceive the prison system as fair or unfair. The results are put in a table like this:

	Men	Women	Total
Fair	57	32	89
Unfair	3	8	11
Total	60	40	100

The table shows that 57 men and 32 women believe the system is fair, and 3 men and 8 women believe that it is unfair. The chi-square can be used to test the null hypothesis that proportions of men and women are the same in their views of fairness. If the null is kept ("retained"), you conclude "no differences." The table is called a 2 × 2 table. The first "2" consists of the columns for men and women, and the second "2" consists of the rows for fair and unfair. Chi-square tests can be expanded to include more rows and columns.

The t test is also used to test for differences. It allows you to compare the average means of two groups to determine the probability that any differences between them are real and not due to chance. You should have at least 20-30 respondents per group and continuous data to use a t test. You need continuous data to calculate the arithmetic average or mean.

Example: t Test

Hope Hospital has initiated a gourmet meal plan. Charity Hospital says gourmet meals cost too much. Do the two hospitals differ in their patients' satisfaction with meals? The surveyors use the Satisfaction Scale (1 = little satisfaction to 10 = much satisfaction). They also ask if any observed differences are statistically meaningful.

The Mann-Whitney U test (also called the Wilcoxon rank sum) enables you to compare two independent groups when you cannot use the t test, for example, when the sample size is too small. This statistical method is a test of the equality of the medians.

Example: Mann-Whitney U Test

Partridge Elementary School had ten fourth-grade students with severe hearing impairments. Four of the students were in a new program to teach them to speak more clearly. At the end of one semester, students in the new program were compared with six students in the traditional program. A special education expert rated each child's ability to speak on a scale from 1 to 20, with 20 representing clear speech. If more students had been available, the surveyor might have chosen the t test to compare the two groups, but after considering the smallness of the sample size, he decided to use the Mann-Whitney U test.

Group means can also be tested with ANOVA, and this method lets you compare several groups (Hope, Charity, and Faith Hospitals or just Hope and Charity Hospitals) at the same time.

Risks and odds are used to describe the likelihood that a particular outcome will occur within a group, or they can be used to compare groups. Suppose that for every 100 persons who have a cold, 20 people also have a cough. The risk of a cough with a cold is 20/100 or .20. The odds of having a cough with a cold is calculated by comparing the number of persons with (20) and without (80) coughs or 20/80, which is .25.

When you use risks and odds to compare groups, you compare the *relative* likelihood that an outcome will take place. The relative risk expresses the risk of a particular outcome in the experimental group relative to the risk of the outcome in the control group. The odds ratio is a description of the comparison of the odds of the outcome in the experimental group with the odds in the control group. You can use the relative risk or the odds ratio with 2×2 tables. Look at this:

Example: Odds Ratio and Relative Risk

Outcome	Experimental	Control
Still smoking		
Quit smoking		

You can ask: What are the odds of still smoking (or quitting) in the experimental group compared to the control? What is the risk of still smoking (or quitting) in the experimental group relative to the risk of still smoking (or quitting) in the control?

The relative risk and the odds ratio will be less than 1 when an outcome occurs less frequently in the experimental than in the control group. Similarly, both will be greater than 1 if the outcome occurs more frequently in the experimental than in the control group.

Why use the odds ratio or relative risk? Why not stay with chi-square? The answer is the confidence interval. Confidence intervals can be placed around odds ratios and relative risks (but not chi-squares), accomplishing the same objective as a significance test. That is, you can determine (by looking at the intervals) if the results are statistically significant.

4. Changes. Special forms of *t* tests and ANOVAs can be used to measure change over time. A dependent *t* test measures change in a single group from Time 1 to Time 2. A repeated measures ANOVA can be used to detect changes in one or more groups at two or more times.

With the McNemar test, each person acts as his or her own control, and small samples and categorical data are used. For example, you can use a McNemar test to find out if a difference exists in the number of students who do and do not choose careers in software engineering after they have participated in a counseling program.

PUTTING THE HORSE IN FRONT OF THE CART: SELECTING ANALYSIS METHODS

The appropriate analysis method for survey data depends on sample size, the survey's research design, and the characteristics and quality of the data. If someone asks, "What is the best method for analyzing survey data?" reply with seven questions that must be answered first:

1. *How Many People Are You Surveying?* Sample size is an important consideration in selecting an analytic strategy. Some statistical methods (*t* tests and ANOVA) depend on relatively larger samples than some other methods such as the Mann-Whitney *U* test. Look at these samples:

A. All 500 teachers in the school district.
B. A stratified sample of 50 teachers in the school district. The strata or divisions are men and women, and high school, junior high school, and elementary school teachers.
C. Six teachers in Hart High School and five in James High School.

Ask: Do you have sufficient data to compute more than tallies, averages, and the variation? You would for Example A, but you probably could not for Example C.

What about Example B? Suppose you were surveying a population of teachers of whom about 60% were women and 40% were men. If you took a sample of 50, and your stratification method were a success, you would have 30 (60% women × 50) in one group, and 20 (40% × 50) men in the other. Groups of 30 and 20 are just about large enough for a *t* test.

Consider this:

	Number of Teachers	
	Men	*Women*
Elementary school	2	15
Middle school	3	10
High school	15	5
Total	20	30

If you want to compare men and women teachers in elementary school, you will have only 2 men and 15 women for your analysis (although for the total, you have 20 men and 30 women). This leads to the second of the seven questions to ask when selecting analysis methods.

2. *Are You Looking for Relationships or Associations?*

Example: Relationships and Associations

A. What is the relationship between voters' political views (as expressed on the Political View Survey) and number of years of formal schooling? The Political View Survey gives continuous scores ranging from 10 (liberal) to 100 (conservative).
B. Are high scores on the Political View Survey associated with high scores on the Authoritarian-Libertarian Inventory? How about medium and low scores?

In the first example, the degree of association between the two variables, political view scores and number of years of formal schooling, can be computed by using the Pearson product-moment correlation because continuous data are available. For the second example, with ranks of high, medium, and low, the Spearman rank-order correlation is appropriate.

3. *Will You Be Comparing Groups?*

Example: Comparing Groups

A. Fifteen teachers in Hart High School will be compared with 20 in James High School.
B. A total of 100 male and female teachers from the district's high schools, junior high schools, and elementary schools will be surveyed in December and June and compared at both times.

If you are comparing groups, statistical tests such as the chi-square, Mann-Whitney *U, t* test, ANOVA, and McNemar tests can help you decide if any observed differences are due to some real occurrence, or if they result from chance or some other factor.

4. *Will Your Survey Be Conducted Once or Several Times?* This question is to find out whether the survey design is cross-sectional or longitudinal.

Example: Looking for Change

A. All 500 teachers will be surveyed in December.
B. A sample of 100 teachers will be surveyed in December and again in June.

Here is a way to display the results of surveys conducted several times:

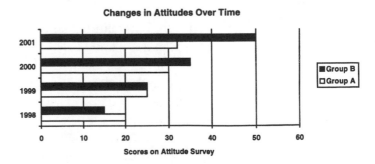

The graph shows that in 1998, Group B had lower scores than Group A. By 2001, Group B had passed Group A. Both groups increased their scores over time. Are the differences between groups significant? Are the differences over time significant? The graph cannot tell us. For statistical significance you need statistical methods.

Here is another way to display changes over time using the same data:

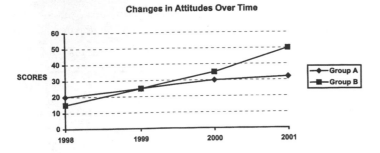

This line graph enables you to visually inspect the slope at which the scores changed. But like the bar graph, you cannot tell just from looking at the graph whether and to what extent the changes are significant.

---

5. *Are the Data Recorded as Numbers and Percentages or Scores and Averages?* Look at this:

A. One set of survey data consists of the number and percentage of teachers who agree or disagree with statements about the district's educational policies.
B. One set of data consists of scores on a measure of attitudes (liberal vs. conservative) to various approaches toward education.

Survey data can be in numbers and percentages (categorical data) or scores that are amenable to the computation of averages (continuous data). The analytic techniques you use with each are different. Look at Tables 6.1 and 6.2.

Comparing numbers of people who were accepted into law school from different programs (categorical data) and comparing the mean scores on an attitude inventory (continuous data) require different analysis techniques. The first comparison might use the chi-square, for example, whereas the second might use a *t* test.

6. *How Many Independent and Dependent Variables Interest You?*

TABLE 6.1 Comparing Men and Women Accepted Into Law School: The Numbers

	Coaching Program A (N = 102)		Coaching Program B (N = 206)	
	n	%	n	%
Men	50	49	100	49
Women	52	51	106	51

TABLE 6.2 Comparing Scores of Men and Women Accepted Into Law School: The Mean

	Coaching Program A (N = 102)		Coaching Program B (N = 106)	
	$\bar{X}$[a]	SD[b]	$\bar{X}$	SD
Men	20.6[c]	2.3	42.8	2.9
Women	15.7	1.4	40.2	2.1

a. Mean.
b. Standard deviation.
c. Scores range from 10 = low to 50 = high.

A variable is a characteristic of interest to your survey. Health status, attitude toward school, self-efficacy, group (experimental, control), gender, job satisfaction, and quality of life are all variables. Independent variables are used to predict or explain findings. They usually include demographics (such as age, ethnicity, gender, income, and whether the respondent is in an experimental or a control group). Dependent variables are what you are looking for in your survey: knowledge, attitudes, behavior.

Suppose you want to know if men and women differ in their quality of life. The independent variable is gender (men and women) and the dependent variable is quality of life. If you want to compare men and women in their quality of life and health status, you will have one independent variable (gender) and two dependent variables (quality of life and health status). You add an independent variable when you ask: How do men and women in the experimental and control teams compare in their quality of life and health status? The added independent variable is team (experimental and control).

You need to know the number of independent and dependent variables to select an appropriate analysis method. Listen to this:

Surveyor: I want to compare two groups of college seniors to find out their lifestyle preferences. There are over 300 in each group.

Analyst: What do you mean by lifestyle preferences? Are you planning to compare numbers of seniors who prefer certain styles of life, say, rural versus urban? Or are you comparing their scores on a survey?

Surveyor:	Seniors in both groups have completed LIFEQUEST, a 100-item survey. It produces scores from 1 to 100. Higher scores are better.
Analyst:	If you have scores on a continuum, you have continuous data. With two groups and continuous data, a *t* test sounds right.
Surveyor:	What method would be correct if I decided to compare numbers?
Analyst:	Chi-square.
Surveyor:	Suppose I had more than two groups and continuous data?
Analyst:	ANOVA.

7. *Are the Data High Quality?*

Data are high quality if the survey is reliable and valid, administered to the right number of the right people, and entered (into the computer) accurately. If the data are incomplete and untruthful, it probably does not matter which analysis method you use because the results won't mean much. If in doubt, keep the analysis simple.

A TECHNICAL INTERLUDE

Here are some common statistical techniques.

Tallies or Frequency Counts

A tally or frequency count is a computation of how many people fit into a category (e.g., 20 are over 55 years of age; 150 have a cold) or choose a response (e.g., 32 said definitely very important; 8 said more than three times a week).

Consider this:

Fifty preschools are surveyed. All are publicly supported. The following question was asked of each school director.

Example: Preschool Purposes Questionnaire

Following are some possible objectives of preschool education. Circle how important each is in guiding your school's program.

Purposes	1. Definitely Important	2. Important	3. Neither Important nor Unimportant	4. Unimportant	5. Definitely Unimportant
To encourage creativity through music, dance, the arts	1	2	3	4	5
To foster academic achievement in reading, math, and science	1	2	3	4	5
To promote good citizenship	1	2	3	4	5
To enhance social and personal development	1	2	3	4	5

For the preschool purposes question, you can tally the responses as shown in the following example:

Example: Tallying Questionnaire Responses

Purpose	*No. and % of Preschool Directors (N = 50) Choosing This Purpose*	
Purpose	*n*	*%*
Academic achievement	20	40
Creativity	13	26
Citizenship	11	22
Social and personal development	6	12

Tallies and frequencies take the form of numbers and percentages. Sometimes you want to group the responses together (or, in technical terms, prepare a frequency distribution of grouped responses), as shown in the next example:

Example: Grouped Ratings of Preschool Purposes by 50 Directors

Number of Directors Choosing This Purpose

Purpose	Definitely Important or Important *n*	Definitely Unimportant or Unimportant *n*
Academic achievement	40	0
Creativity	15	30
Citizenship	26	5
Social and personal development	7	42
Total	88	77

In this table, the responses are divided into two ("dichotomized"): important (including two categories of response: definitely important and important) and not important (including two categories of responses: definitely unimportant and unimportant). Why group responses? If only a few respondents select one of the choices (e.g., only three answer definitely important), then the category may lose its meaning to you. Grouping may be confusing to the reader who may not know just how few people actually chose definitely important.

Averages: Means, Medians, and Modes

The mean, median, and mode are all measures of average or typical performance.

The Mean. The arithmetic average, the mean, requires summing units and dividing by the number of units you have added together. Here are five scores: 50, 30, 24, 10, 6.

The average for these five scores is 50 + 30 + 24 + 10 + 6 divided by 5 = 24.

The formula for the mean is

$$\mu_x = \frac{\Sigma X}{N}$$

The symbol for the mean is μ, and Σ stands for the sum, so ΣX means to add all the numerical values such as X. N stands for the number of Xs.

Suppose you wanted to compute the average rating for the four preschool purposes. First you'd have to know how many directors assigned each rating to each purpose (see Table 6.3).

To compute the average rating for each purpose, you would multiply the number of directors who chose each point on the scale times the value of the scale. For creativity, for example, 13 directors chose a 1, so you would multiply 13 by 1, add the results together $(13 \times 1) + (2 \times 2) + (5 \times 3) + (20 \times 4) + (10 \times 5)$ and divide by the number of directors: 13 + 4 + 15 + 80 + 50 divided by 50 = 3.24, the average rating for creativity.

In this case, the closer the averages are to 1, the more important the purpose (see Table 6.4).

The Median. The median is the point on a scale that has an equal number of scores above and below it. Another way of putting it is that the median is at the 50th percentile. Because the median always falls in the middle, it is used when you want to describe typical performance.

Why do you need typical performance? Suppose you had a set of scores like this: 5, 5, 6, 6, 6, 8, 104.

The average is 20, the median is 6. How can this happen? It may if the group you were sampling was divided in its attitude (or knowledge or health, etc.), with most people feeling one way and some feeling much different. It can also happen if you are unable to collect all the data you plan to, and many of the people with one view are not represented in the responses. Here is how to compute the median if you have an equal number of scores:

1. Arrange the scores in order of size.
2. Place the median between the $N/2$ score and the $(N/2) + 1$ score (where N equals the number of scores), using the arithmetic average.

TABLE 6.3 Ratings of 50 Preschool Directors

	1. Definitely Important	2. Important	3. Neither Important nor Unimportant	4. Unimportant	5. Definitely Unimportant
Academic achievement	26	20	4	0	0
Creativity	13	2	5	20	10
Citizenship	11	24	10	10	0
Social and personal development	6	1	1	30	12

TABLE 6.4 Average Importance Ratings Assigned by 50 Preschool Directors

Purpose	Average
Academic achievement	1.56
Citizenship	2.18
Creativity	3.24
Social and personal development	3.82

Example: Computing the Median for Even Number of Scores

Take these scores: –2, 0, 6, 7, 9, 9.

There are six scores, so $N = 6$, with $N/2 = 3$ and $(N/2) + 1 = 4$.

The third score in order equals 6, and the fourth equals 7, so the median is 6.5.

Take these scores: 2, 4, 5, 8, 9, 11.

Again $N = 6$, so the median is between the third and fourth scores, 5 and 8. This time, however, there is a gap of 3 units between the third and fourth scores. Adding the two scores 5 + 8 and dividing by 2 gives a value of 6.5 for the median.

When a set of data is small and odd in number:

1. Arrange the scores in order of size.
2. Place the median at the score that is the $(N + 1)/2$ from the bottom of the distribution.

Example: Computing the Median for an Odd Number of Scores

Try these: –9, –8, –6, –6, –4, –3, –2, 0, 2

The median of these nine scores is $(9 + 1)/2$ or the fifth score, and so the median is –4.

But suppose that in either an even-numbered or odd-numbered set of cases, you have several identical scores at the median or bordering it, as with this set: 3, 6, 7, 8, 8, 8, 9, 9, 10, 12.

When $N = 10$, as in this case, the median would usually fall between the fifth and sixth score. Calling 8 the median this time will not work because you need five different scores above and five different scores below.

But if you consider a score of 8 as part of a continuum that is evenly spread throughout the interval between 7.5 and 8.5, you can interpolate and come up with an intermediate score.

Think of it this way:

You have three cases (3, 6, 7) until you come to the interval of 7.5 to 8.5, which contains three 8s. Within that interval you will need two more cases to make a total of 5. So, you add two-thirds of the distance or .67 to 7.5, and you get a median of 8.17.

The Mode. The mode is a score (or a point on the score scale) that has a higher frequency than other scores in its vicinity. Look at these scores:

Distribution A		Distribution B	
Score	Frequency	Score	Frequency
34	2	34	0
33	6	33	1
32	8	32	7
31	11	31	11
30	15	30	4
29	18	29	3
28	16	28	7
27	12	27	10
26	8	26	18
25	3	25	23
24	1	24	11
23	0	23	5

Distribution A has a single mode of 29, with 18 people getting that score. This distribution is called unimodal. Distribution B has two modes, at 25 and 31, so the distribution is bimodal. (Although the frequency of 11 associated with the score of 31 is the same or lower than that of other scores, the score is a mode because it has a higher frequency than the others near it.)

The mode, with its concentration of scores, describes the prevailing view. You might use the mode when you suspect that you have a group with widely differing characteristics. For example, if you suspect that the reason people in Social Action Program D did better than those in Program C is because they were economically better off to begin with, you might compare their incomes before they entered each program.

If you find something like this, you could conclude that you are probably right:

People in Program D are on the high-income part of the scale, and those in Program C are on the

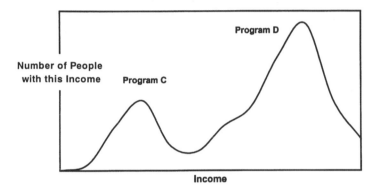

low-income side. Groups C and D together give you a bimodal distribution.

Variation: Range, Variance, and Standard Deviation

When you compute an arithmetic average, every number counts. If one or two people have very high or low scores, they can make the average seem artificially higher or lower. Using the median helps, but it, too, can be misleading. Consider this set of scores: 2, 3, 4, 5, 6, 7, 8.

The mean and median are 5. If you were to change the last two scores to 17 and 18, the median would stay the same at 5, with three cases above and below the score. The mean would rise to 55/7 = 7.86.

If every number counts, it is sometimes important to study the spread of scores—their variation—to

TABLE 6.5   Attendance at 60 Continuing Education Classes

School	No. of Teachers	Average No. of Classes Attended	Range
1	50	55.0	16-60
2	103	54.0	53-60
3	86	41.0	15-59
4	117	47.5	15-60

shed light on how the mean came to be what it is. Are all the scores near the arithmetic average? Are some very high or very low? Look at Table 6.5.

If you look at the average number of classes attended at the four schools, you find that it is 49.4. Looking farther, you see that at some schools, as few as 15 classes were attended, whereas at others, all 60 were. In fact, it is hard not to be struck by the range of attendance. At least several inferences can be made because you have access to the range.

1. Variation existed in three of the four schools (1, 3, and 4), with some teachers attending many classes and others attending very few.
2. In only one school (2) did almost everyone attend about the same number of classes as everyone else.

In some cases, variation is considered an asset. A program to train people to think independently or creatively might expect a survey to reveal a variety of perspectives. You also need variation to make comparisons. If everyone performs equally well or shares the same views, you cannot select the best, the strongest, the most liberal or conservative, and so on. In other cases, however, variation is a disappointment because you want everyone to share the same view or achieve a skill at the same level of proficiency. If the district that is sponsoring the continuing education believes its programs are worthwhile, the wide range of attendance will be disappointing.

Another measure of variation is called the variance, and its square root is called the standard deviation. This is a statistical term based on a score's distance from the mean. In fact, the standard deviation is the average distance the average score is from the mean.

The formula for the standard deviation (*SD*) is

$$SD = \sqrt{\frac{\Sigma(X - \overline{X})^2}{n - 1}}$$

Suppose you had the following scores on the Self-Assessment Survey: 7, 10, 8, 5, 4, 8, 4, 9, 7, 8. Here is how you would get the standard deviation.

1. Compute the mean:

$$\overline{X} = \frac{(7 + 10 + 8 + 5 + 4 + 8 + 4 + 9 + 7 + 8)}{10} = 7.$$

2. Subtract each score (*X*) from the mean ($\overline{X}$) or $X - \overline{X}$.

3. Square the remainder from Step 2, or $(X - \overline{X})^2$.

	Step 2	Step 3
Score	$(X - \overline{X})$	$(X - \overline{X})^2$
7	(7 – 7) = 0	0
10	(10 – 7) = 3	9
8	(8 – 7) = 1	1
5	(5 – 7) = –2	4
4	(4 – 7) = –3	9
8	(8 – 7) = 1	1
4	(4 – 7) = –3	9
9	(9 – 7) = 2	4
7	(7 – 7) = 0	0
8	(8 – 7) = 1	1

4. Sum up (Σ) all the remainders from Step 3, or $\Sigma (X - \overline{X})^2$:

$$\Sigma(X - \overline{X})^2 = 0 + 9 + 1 + 4 + 9 + 1 + 9 + 4 + 1 = 38.$$

5. Divide the number in Step 4 by $n - 1$ (*n* is the number of scores):

$$\frac{38}{n - 1} = \frac{38}{9} = 4.22.$$

6. Take the square root of the result of Step 5:

$$\sqrt{4.22} = 2.05 .$$

Like the range, the standard deviation is a calculation describing the spread of scores. You will often see the standard deviation in tables of data where means are given. Sometimes instead of the standard deviation, the variance is used. The variance is simply the square of the standard deviation, or the result of Step 5 (4.22).

You can compute the variance and standard deviation on data only from continuous data such as average scores. Variation in categorical data (from nominal and ordinal scales) is best expressed in terms of the range.

Pearson Product-Moment Correlation Coefficient

Correlations measure the relationship between two variables. They are reported within a range of +1 (perfect positive correlation) to –1 (perfect negative correlation).

When high values on one variable occur simultaneously with high values on another, the two variables are said to be positively correlated, and when high values on one variable occur with low values on another, the two variables are said to be negatively correlated.

The correlation coefficient is symbolized as *r* and is usually reported to two decimal places. The formula for calculating *r* is

$$r = \frac{\Sigma(X - \overline{X}) \, (Y - \overline{Y})}{\sqrt{\Sigma(X - \overline{X})^2} \; \sqrt{\Sigma(Y - \overline{Y})^2}} .$$

Consider the following:

A marketing survey for a women's journal asked two questions: How many magazines its readers received from subscriptions each month and their number of years of education. A correlation was computed to see if these two variables (number of monthly subscriptions and years of education) were correlated.

Here is how to calculate the correlation coefficient. *X* is the independent variable (years of education). *Y* is the dependent variable, and it refers to number of magazine subscriptions each month. Ten people participate in the survey.

1. Using Table 6.6 to get each Σ in the formula, you see that

$$\Sigma(X - \overline{X}) \, (Y - \overline{Y}) = 101.$$

$$\Sigma(X - \overline{X})^2 \, (Y - \overline{Y})^2 = 101.1 \times 103.$$

TABLE 6.6 Correlation Coefficient: Ten Respondents

Respondent	X	Y	$X - \bar{X}\ (\bar{X} = 9.5)$	$Y - \bar{Y}\ (\bar{Y} = 11.8)$	$(X - \bar{X})(Y - \bar{Y})$	$(X - \bar{X})^2$	$(Y - \bar{Y})^2 t$
a	10	12	.5	.2	.1	.2	.04
b	12	14	2.5	2.2	5.5	6.2	4.8
c	5	7	–4.5	–4.8	21.6	20.2	23.0
d	7	9	–2.5	–2.8	7.0	6.2	7.8
e	7	10	–2.5	–1.8	4.5	6.2	3.2
f	12	15	2.5	3.2	8.0	6.2	10.2
g	10	13	.5	1.2	.6	.2	1.4
h	6	8	–3.5	–3.8	13.3	12.2	14.4
i	10	12	.5	.2	.1	.2	.04
j	16	18	6.5	6.2	40.3	42.3	38.4
Sum	95	118			101	100.1	103.3

2. Filling in the formula, you get

   a. 101/100.1 × 103.3
      100.1 = 10 (rounded)
      103.3 = 10.2 (rounded)
   b. 101/10 × 10.2
      10 × 10.2 = 102
   c. 101/102 = .99

The correlation coefficient is .99, suggesting a nearly perfect relationship between years of education and monthly magazine subscriptions.

Warning: You can use correlations to identify relationships between variables, but you cannot use them to establish causation. A correlation analysis can show that people who have completed many years of schooling usually subscribe to many magazines, but it cannot show that people subscribe because they had many years of schooling.

Analysis of Variance (ANOVA)

If you want to compare two or more groups or study changes that take place in the same group from one time to the next, ANOVA is a method you should consider. Here is how to proceed.

1. *Make Sure ANOVA Is Appropriate.* Remember, ANOVA is used to test for differences among groups or across times. Here are examples of questions that can be answered using one-way ANOVA:

Question 1: Do patients in the experimental program have different mean satisfaction scores than do patients in the traditional program?

Question 2: Do boys and girls in three different reading programs differ in their attitudes toward school? Attitude data are continuous and come from the ASQ (Attitude Toward School Questionnaire).

2. *State Your Hypothesis.* In Question 1, for example, you will test the equality of experimental and control groups to learn about satisfaction. First, you have to rephrase the questions as a hypothesis. You will be tempted to do this:

Tempting hypothesis: On the average, patients in the experimental program and patients in the traditional program are different in their mean satisfaction.

Preferred hypothesis: Patients in the experimental and control program are the same (or do not differ) in their mean satisfaction.

ANOVA cannot directly prove that there are differences among groups. It can prove only that they are not the same. To use ANOVA properly, you must test hypotheses about the sameness or equality of behavior and not the differences. The equality of means (remember, in ANOVA you test the equality of means) is called the null hypothesis.

3. *Make Sure You Have the Data You Need in the Form You Need.* ANOVA depends on the use of

arithmetic averages and standard deviations. You cannot use ANOVA to test a hypothesis about the equality of two groups' behavior unless you have a way to determine their mean performance. This suggests that your survey uses scales that produce continuous data so that you can calculate the mean.

4. *Test the Hypotheses and Report the Results.* Hypotheses are tested with an F statistic, which is derived mathematically using the ANOVA formula. The null hypothesis for the F test is that group variances are equal. The variance is the standard deviation squared.

Table A2 in the appendix contains the F distribution. This table lists the smallest value that an F statistic can take for you to reject a hypothesis. These tables provide F values for different degrees of freedom (df) and significance levels (p). Degrees of freedom are the number of independent scores (or observations) entering into the computation of the statistic. The level of significance refers to the probability of falsely rejecting the hypothesis. Surveyors usually use the .05 or .01 significance level, which means that there are either 5 chances in 100 or 1 chance in 100 that the hypothesis will be rejected unintentionally.

Look at this computer output for an ANOVA:

Example: Portion of a Typical Output for a One-Way Analysis of Variance (ANOVA)

Page 3 STAT-PC 04/05/—

ONE-WAY ANOVA

Source	DF	Sums of Squares	Mean Squares	F Ratio	F Prob.
Among groups	2	248.0000	124.0000	8.9793	.0020
Within groups[a]	18	248.5714	13.8095		
Total	20	496.5714			

a. Some programs call this "error."

This is a sample output for a one-way ANOVA. It is one way because there is only one independent variable (group), although there are three subgroups. Part 1 of the output includes a description of two sources of variation. Remember, the F test checks the equality of variances among groups (in this example, 3) and within each group. The F ratio is the statistic you get when you divide the among-groups mean square by the within-groups mean square (sometimes called the error variance). The F probability is the observed significance level: the probability of obtaining an F statistic at least as large as the one calculated when all population means are equal.

ANOVA compares the variation between each respondent and the respondent's group mean (within groups) and the variation between each group mean and the grand mean. The grand mean is the mean of all the individual group means. If Group A has a mean of 50 and Group B has a mean of 100, the grand mean is 50 plus 100 or 150 divided by 2, which is 75. If the observed probability is small enough, the hypothesis that all populations means are equal can be rejected. With the probability of .0020 shown in the output, it is unlikely that the groups are the same. When the output provides the probability, you do not have to look at a table. Some programs just give the F ratio. With these, you must use a table to decide whether to accept or reject the null. If you set the significance level at .01, for 2 degrees of freedom for the numerator (the rows in the table) and 20 (for the columns), the value in the table is 6.01. Because the observed value is greater than the obtained value, the three means are not equal and the null is rejected.

t Test

The t distribution is used to test hypotheses about the mean (so you need continuous data). The shape of the t distribution approaches the shape of a standard normal distribution as its sample size approaches 30. A standard normal distribution is bell shaped. A typical normal distribution has a mean of 0 and a standard deviation of 1.

Here are three situations in which a t test may be used.

Example: *t* Test in Three Situations

1. *Client Satisfaction*
Employees at the Internext Network's scored a mean of 35.6. How does this compare to WorldOver's mean score? To make the comparison between groups, use an independent t test.
2. *Food Preferences*

Do average scores on the Good Food Inventory change after patients participate in a cholesterol-lowering program? To compare patients before and after they participate in the program, use a dependent *t* test.

3. *Clothing Prices*

The Price Survey found that women in the county of Thousand Palms spend an average of $150 each time they shop for clothing. How does this average compare with the national survey results? To compare the means obtained by women in Thousand Palms and the national means, use a one-sample *t* test. In this survey, the mean of a group is compared with a norm or standard: the national results.

A *t* test must meet certain assumptions to be used. For the independent *t* test, you need to satisfy two. Remember, an independent *t* test hypothesizes no difference between two groups whose survey results are given as continuous data. The first assumption to be fulfilled is that the data are normally distributed. How do you find out if the data are normal? The good news is that many computer programs will plot survey data for you so you can make this determination visually. But the data also need to meet a second assumption: The variances of the two samples also must be equal. The *F* statistic (same as the one for ANOVA) is used to test this assumption. Again, you are likely to find the results of this test on the output.

If the data do not meet these assumptions, you can "transform" the data or change its scale, or consider using nonparametric statistical methods that do not make assumptions about the distribution. The method to use to test for the difference between two paired samples is the Wilcoxon signed-ranks test. It actually tests the hypothesis that the medians (not the means) are equal. If you have independent samples, use the Wilcoxon rank-sum test (also called the Mann-Whitney *U*). It also tests the equality of the medians.

Here is an example of the computer output for an independent-samples *t* test.

Example: Computer Output—Independent Samples *t* Test

Global Tech is concerned that its employees are not participating in the firm's preventive health care activities as often as they should. Absenteeism is on the rise slightly, and Global is concerned that it may be health related but preventable. The Human Resources Department conducts a survey to compare employees who use the Fitness Center more than once a week with those who use it once a week or less. The survey focuses on perceptions of physical health and well-being.

Type of survey: Computer-based survey (on disk)
Survey questions

- How often in the past 12 months did you use the Fitness Center?
  Once a week or less (yes, no)
  More than once a week (yes, no)

- The Physical Functioning Inventory (PFI) has ten questions. A score of 100 means highest physical functioning.

Distribution:	Normal
Independent variable:	Use of the center (more than once a week versus once a week or less)
Dependent variable:	Physical functioning (score on the PFI)
Analysis method:	*t* test
Output	

Page 3	STATUS +	6/13/—

Independent Samples of Q41L — USE CENTER

Group 1: Q41 1.00[a]   Group 2: 2.00[b]

t test for PFI scores:

	Number of Cases[c]	Mean[d]	Standard Deviation[e]	Standard Error[f]
Group 1	561	75.5261	23.957	1.011
Group 2	311	77.4358	24.112	1.367

Pooled Variance Estimate[i]				Separate Variance Estimate[j]			
F Value[g]	2-Tail Probability[h]	t Value	Degrees of Freedom	2-Tail Probability	t Value	Degrees of Freedom	2-Tail Probability
1.01	.890	−1.13	870	261	−1.12	636.61	.262

Interpretation

a. Group 1 chose "yes": Used the center more than once a week. Their code is 1.00 for this group.
b. Group 2 answered "yes": Used the center once a week or less. Their code is 2.00.
c. Number of cases refers to the number of employees who answered the survey (sample size) in each group.
d. Mean score obtained on the PFI by each group.
e. Standard deviation of the scores.
f. Standard error of the means.
g. The *F* value or statistic obtained in the test to determine the equality of the variances.
h. Probability of obtaining a result like the *F* value if the null (no difference between groups) is true. If the obtained probability is less than some agreed-on alpha like .05 or .01, the null is rejected. In this case, the probability of .890 is greater than .05, and so the null is retained. The conclusion is that no differences exist in the variances of the two groups.
i. The pooled variance estimate is used when variances are equal. The *p* value is .261, greater than an alpha of .05. The null hypothesis regarding the equality of the group means is retained.
j. The separate variance is used when variances are not equal.

Conclusion

No differences exist in physical functioning between employees who use the center more than once a week in the past 12 months and those who use it once a week or less.

Chi-Square (χ^2) for Two Independent Samples

This is an example of chi-square in use:

Example: Chi-Square

MEDEX is a program designed to encourage high school students to pursue careers in health. The school board commis-

sioned an evaluation to see if MEDEX was a success. As part of the evaluation, 210 high school seniors were randomly selected. Half received MEDEX and the other half did not. All 210 students were then surveyed at the end of the school year to learn about their vocational preferences. At that time, two of the students in the no-MEDEX group were disqualified from the evaluation when they enrolled in another program similar to MEDEX.

The evaluators organized the data into a table and used a chi-square statistic to test whether interest in careers in health was the same in both groups.

Group 1	Group 2	Total
A	B	A + B
C	D	C + D
A + C	B + D	n = A + C + B + D

This is a formula you can use for this 2 × 2 table:

$$\chi^2 = \frac{n(A \times D) - (B \times C)^2}{(A + B)(C + D)(A + C)(B + D)}$$

The formula was applied to the MEDEX experiment:

No MEDEX	MEDEX
103	105

Career Preference	No MEDEX	MEDEX	Total
No health	80	30	110
Health	23	75	98
Total	103	105	208

$$\chi^2 = \frac{208\,[(80 \times 75) - (213 \times 30)]^2}{(103)(105)(110)(98)}$$

$$= 48.35.$$

The evaluators used a table to find out the significance of a chi-square value of 48.35 with 1 degree of freedom (which you get with a 2-by-2 table). (See the appendix.) The differences between groups were found to be statistically significant at the .01 level. The evaluators concluded that participating in MEDEX probably makes a difference in encouraging students to consider careers in health.

STATISTICAL SIGNIFICANCE

Suppose you survey the attitudes of two groups of students, one of which is in an experimental reading program. Also suppose that the experimental group's scores are much poorer than the other group's, say, by 10 points. Are the relatively poorer scores due to chance or is the new reading program responsible? Anything that is unlikely to happen by chance can be called statistically significant. How much of a difference between the two groups is necessary before you can eliminate chance as the motivation?

To determine statistical significance, you must rely on sampling theory. For example, you ask a question such as: What is the probability that my two random samples of students from the same population will produce mean scores that differ by as much as, say, 10 points? 20 points?

Suppose you decide that a chance happening of 1 time in 100 is an acceptable risk. This predefined probability ($p < .01$) is called the level of significance. If the differences you observe occur no more than 1 out of 100 times, you can reject the null hypothesis of no difference between groups.

Surveyors usually use the .05, .01, and .001 significance levels, meaning that the observed difference in the experimental and traditional programs will be considered statistically significant if the difference of 10 points would occur by chance (assuming the two groups are random samples from the same population) only 5 times in 100, 1 time in 100, or 1 time in 1,000.

Understanding Type I and Type II Errors

In testing statistical hypotheses, you must establish rules that determine when you will accept or reject a null hypothesis. The null hypothesis tests the proposition that the groups are the same or, put another way, no differences exist between (or among) groups.

Take, for example, a statistical test of an experimental (A) and control (B) reading program, where the null hypothesis is that the mean reading scores for both groups are equal.

When you apply a statistical test (such as the t test) to the data, you do not expect to find zero differences in mean scores between the two groups. Instead, the real question is whether the differences are so small that they could have occurred simply by chance. When you select two random samples from the same population, you can expect their mean scores to be close, but not exactly the same.

It is up to you to decide how far apart the scores must be before you are satisfied that the difference is not just an accident. You could choose .10, .05, .01, or .001 as the level of significance, depending on the amount of error you are willing to tolerate in rejecting the null hypothesis.

If you select the .05 level of significance, then about 5 times in 100 you will reject the null hypothesis when it is, in fact, correct. This happens because you are comparing two random samples from the same population, and the probability that they will differ by chance alone is 5% ($p < .05$). This situation is known as a Type I error. It is the probability of rejecting the null hypothesis when it is true.

If the level of significance is .01, then the probability of a Type I error is only 1 in 100, or 1%. You can select a level of significance that would virtually eliminate the chance of a Type I error, but there are serious consequences. The less likely you are to make a Type I error, the more likely you are to make a Type II error.

A Type II error is when you accept a null hypothesis that is, in fact, incorrect. In that case, the difference between the two groups' mean scores does not fall within the rejection region (say, $p < .05$). But in reality, the groups are not alike and the experimental treatment is better (the alternative hypothesis is true).

The power of a statistical test is the probability of correctly rejecting the null hypothesis. Mathematically, power is equal to Type I minus Type II error. From that formula, you can see that Type I errors, Type II errors, and power are interrelated. As the probability of making a Type I error decreases, the probability of making a Type II error increases, but the power of the statistical test decreases.

In statistical testing, you weigh the consequences and decide in advance which risk to take. Is it better to risk declaring the experimental group the victor when there is actually no difference between them (a Type I error)? Or is it better to risk saying there is no difference when the experimental group is really better (a Type II error)?

Because statistically significant results seem to be regarded as a research "finding" more often than insignificant results, Type I errors are more likely to find their way into print.

Notice that the output for ANOVA (see the earlier section example: Portion of a Typical Output for a One-Way Analysis of Variance) reports the F probability as .0020. Most statistical programs can automatically provide the exact p value such as .0020 (rather than $p < .01$) or .03 (rather than $p < .05$). It is recommended that you report the exact value of p. Like the confidence interval, it can provide additional and more precise information about the obtained difference.

Confidence Intervals and p Values

Look at this portion of the output for an ANOVA:

Example: Differences and Confidence Intervals

Group	Count	Mean	Standard Deviation	Standard Error	95% Conf Int for Mean		
1	7	11.0000	3.6056	1.3628	7.6654	to	14.3346
2	7	8.1429	4.2984	1.6245	4.1675	to	12.1182
3	7	16.4286	4.9828	1.0873	9.5890	to	14.1253
Total	21	11.8571	4.9828	1.0873	9.5890	to	14.1253

The output contains a table with descriptive statistics: the number of units (the count), the mean, standard deviation, standard error, and the "Conf Int" or confidence interval for the mean. A confidence interval is a range of values within which the true value lies. So for Group 1, you can be confident that 95% of the time the true mean will be between 7.6654 and 14.3346.

You can plot the confidence intervals on a graph. If the intervals do not overlap, differences exist. If the mean of one group is contained in the interval of the second, differences do not exist. If the intervals overlap, but not the means, you cannot tell.

Look at this graph for the ANOVA confidence intervals.

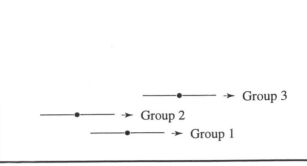

Group 1 Confidence Interval 7.67 to 14.33, $\overline{X} = 11.00$

Group 2 Confidence Interval 4.17 to 12.11, $\overline{X} = 8.14$

Group 3 Confidence Interval 13.51 to 19.35, $\overline{X} = 16.43$

Group 2's mean score is within Group 1's confidence interval. Group 3's interval does not really overlap with either group. Differences in the means can be seen, and you can reject the null (that the means are the same). Also, notice that the exact probability values (see the section example: Portion of a Typical Output for a One-Way Analysis of Variance) and confidence intervals agree in their outcome: The null should be rejected.

The confidence interval and p are related. If the interval contains 0, then the p is not significant. Confidence intervals are regularly used. In fact, they are often preferred in studies of two or more groups because you can see the range of values. A wide range is less conclusive than a narrow one. Compare an interval of means between 1 and 100 and one from 1 to 5. The wider range is less convincing.

Coding for Data Analysis

A code has two components: a number for the response (such as yes = 1 and no = 2) and a number describing which column or space to put a respondent's reply. Here's a portion of a survey and its codes.

Example: Survey Questions and Codes

A. During the past seven days, how many times did you eat six servings of vegetables? *Circle one.*

Once	1	*17*
Two or three times	2	*18*
Four or more	3	*19*

B. In the past week, did you eat any of the following?
Circle one for each choice of vegetable. *Circle one.*

	1. Yes	2. No	
Broccoli	1	2	20
Spinach	1	2	21
Corn	1	2	22
Yams	1	2	23
Potatoes	1	2	24

or

C. Which of these did you eat in the past week?
Check all that apply.

☐ Broccoli   20

☐ Spinach   21

☐ Corn   22

☐ Yams   23

☐ Potatoes   24

☐ I ate none of these   25

_____

The numbers to the right of the questions are the columns or places where the responses to each choice are to be put. To the data enterer, it works this way:

What the Data Enterer Does for Items A, B, and C.

Item A: For each respondent choice, place a 1 for a yes and a 2 for a no.

Item B: In columns 20, 21, 22, and 23, place a 1 or 2, depending on the person's response.

Item C: In columns 20, 21, 22, 23, and 24, place a 1 if checked; place a 2 if not checked.

If an item is left blank, the column must be assigned some number such as 9 (assuming eight or fewer choices). If there are nine choices or more, can you use another code, say, 99? The answer is yes, but then you must provide for data entry into two columns, and the numbers would be entered as 01, 02, . . . 99.

Look at this:

Example: Coding Strips for Items With More Than Nine Choices or With a Double-Digit Answer
_____

D. What was your total household income before taxes in 1993?

☐ $10,000 or less   *20-21*

☐ $10,100 to $12,000

☐ $12,100 to $15,000

☐ $15,100 to $20,000

☐ $21,000 to $30,000

☐ $31,000 to $40,000

☐ $41,000 to $50,000

☐ $51,000 to $70,000

☐ $71,000 to $90,000

☐ Over $90,000

E. How many people in your household are supported by your total household income?

Write in number of household members:

_____   *50-51*

_____

Data Entry

Before entering survey data, you must decide how to file them, or, in other words, how to create a data file. For most statistical analyses, you create a rectangular file or a table. In the rectangular file, each horizontal line contains all the data—the data record—for a particular respondent and each vertical field represents a particular variable (e.g., age). Often, each record in a data file represents individual respondents. Sometimes, however, the record consists of all information for a cluster of individuals or other units like a classroom or school.

Data can be entered into spreadsheets or forms. Spreadsheets are like rectangular files in which rows represent cases or records and columns represent variables. The form uses the whole computer screen for the case that is being entered, and it can be structured to look like the original survey instrument. A programmer can help you create tailor-made forms for data entry. Then you must be sure that data enterers are trained to enter the data quickly and accurately.

The Codebook

A codebook is the historical record of the analytic decisions you have made. If you collapse the categories "definitely important" and "important" and report frequencies on a new category called "important," for example, this should be included in the codebook. Rules for handling missing data, transforming it, and so on should also be included. The codebook is your documentation. If you want to use the survey again, the codebook provides a record of how the data were handled. If someone else wants to duplicate the survey, they should be able to rely on the codebook.

Preparation of the codebook can begin as soon as the analysis plan is agreed on, but it should be made final after the completion of the analysis. At its simplest, the codebook contains a number for each variable, its location (the column in which it can be found), a name for the variable (usually eight or fewer characters in capital letters to accommodate common statistical packages), and a brief description of the meaning of each code.

Here is a portion of a codebook for a data set collected from a survey of very young mothers who participated in a survey about informed consent in cesarean birth deliveries.

Example: Codebook

Variable No.	Variable Location (column)	Variable Name	Description and Comments
1	1-5	PROJID	A five-digit ID project code; use 99999 for missing values.
2	6-9	INDIVID	A four-digit ID individual code; use 9999 for missing values.
3	10-15	DLIVDATE	Enter month/day/year using two digits for each segment. May 20, 2000 = 052000. Use 99 for any missing segment; use 999999 if entire date is missing.
4	16-21	FOLLDATE	Use same procedure as for DLIVDATE.
5	22	POSPARVIS	No = 1, Yes = 2, Don't know = 3, use 9 for missing.
6	23-28	VISTDATE	Follow DLIVDATE procedure. If POSPARVIS = No use 888888/ Use 999999 if missing.
7	36-37	WELVISIT	Use two digits. 1 = 01, 2 = 02, etc. Use 00 if none and 99 if missing.

PRESENTING THE SURVEY RESULTS

OVERVIEW

Survey results can be shown on the survey form itself and in tables, graphs, diagrams, or pictures. This approach shows the survey's raw data.

Survey reports nearly always have tables. Their purpose is to describe respondents and show relationships and changes. Follow the rules if you plan to use tables. For example, use the table's columns to show the independent variables such as group and timing of survey (baseline, six months later, three years later). Select a table format and use it consistently, rely on vertical lines sparingly, and present data in logical order such as from most to least frequent.

Pie diagrams show visually the proportion occupied by each response category. The key to an accurate pie diagram is its scale. Each slice must be equal in proportion to the number or percentage of responses it represents. Bar graphs are commonly used to display survey data because they provide an overview of several kinds of information—comparisons and changes—at one glance. Line graphs also show changes and differences in groups. Be careful not to oversell and make a 1-point change in score look significant unless it really is.

Most surveys result in written reports. Consider including these sections in your report: abstract, summary, table of contents and figures, glossary of terms, statement of purposes or objectives, methods, results, conclusions, recommendations, references, index, appendix, and acknowledgments.

Overheads are effective visual aids in oral survey reports. They are fairly inexpensive to produce and require a simple computer program, access to a copying machine, and special transparency paper. Slides are more expensive and formal. If you use overheads or slides, use one main idea or concept per overhead or slide. If you want immediate feedback on the report, make your presentation directly from the computer.

Survey results can be shown on the survey form itself and in tables, graphs, diagrams, or pictures.

REPRODUCING THE QUESTIONNAIRE

You report the responses to each question directly on the survey form. Set the responses off in some way. Look at this:

Example: Reporting Results With the Questionnaire

---

3. During the *past four weeks,* how much of the time have you felt depressed?

   Mark (X) one box

☐ All of the time	5%
☐ Most of the time	3%
☐ A good bit of the time	8%

☐ Some of the time   *42%*

☐ A little of the time   *32%*

☐ None of the time   *10%*

The advantage of using the survey form is to let the reader or listener know the question and response choices that were given to the respondent. This approach shows the survey's raw data.

USING TABLES

Survey reports nearly always have tables. Their purpose is to describe respondents and show relationships and changes. Look at these two tables:

Example: Describing Respondents in Two Schools

Characteristic	School 1		School 2	
	n	*%*	*n*	*%*
Age in years	___		___	
Grade point average	___		___	
Reading score	___		___	
Mathematics score	___		___	
Science score	___		___	

Example: Comparing Respondents in Two Schools

Characteristic	School 1		School 2		*t*	*p*
	n	*%*	*n*	*%*		
Age in years	___		___		___	___
Grade point average	___		___		___	___
Reading score	___		___		___	___
Mathematics score	___		___		___	___
Science score	___		___		___	___

The first table lists the characteristics (such as age and grade point average) of students in each of the schools. The second table tells you if the differences are statistically significant.

TABLE 7.1   Children With Healthy and Unhealthy Lifestyles[a] in Four Schools

School	Healthy		Unhealthy	
	n	*%*	*n*	*%*
Alameda (*n* = 264)	140	19	124	17
Berkeley (*n* = 152)	100	14	52*	7
Delacorte (*n* = 227)	89	12	138**	18
Santa Inez (*n* = 91)	45	6	46	7
Total (*N* = 734)	374		360	

SOURCE: Self-administered National Children's Health Survey, Center for Health Statistics.
a. Scores of 75 to 100 indicate healthy lifestyles. Scores of 26 to 74 indicate neither healthy nor unhealthy lifestyles. Scores of 1 to 25 indicate unhealthy lifestyles.
$*p = .003$ between healthy and unhealthy within school. $**p = .002$ between healthy and unhealthy within school.

Table 7.1 is another example that shows statistically significant differences (indicated by one and two asterisks). This table also has a source listed: National Children's Health Survey, Center for Health Statistics. Include the source of the information when it is not obvious. The source is not obvious if it comes from anyone but the reporter. Notice, too, that the scores are explained in superscript note a.

Look at Tables 7.2 and 7.3.

TABLE 7.2   Changes in Self-Efficacy (in percentages)

Level	Under 65 Years		65 Years and Older	
	1997 (*n = 128*)	*1998* (*n = 49*)	*1997* (*n = 104*)	*1998* (*n = 212*)
High	0	70	0	69
Medium	57	28	57	31
Low	43	2	43	0

SOURCE: *The Self-Efficacy Scale* (New York: National Press).
NOTE: Scale is 1 to 9, where 1-3 = high and 7-9 = low.

TABLE 7.3   Changes in Self-Efficacy (in percentages)

Level	1997		1998	
	Under 65 Years (*n = 128*)	*65 Years and Older* (*n = 49*)	*Under 65 Years* (*n = 104*)	*65 Years and Older* (*n = 212*)
High	0	0	70	69
Medium	57	57	28	31
Low	43	43	2	0

SOURCE: *The Self-Efficacy Scale* (New York: National Press).
NOTE: Scale is 1 to 9, where 1-3 = high and 7-9 = low.

Which tells you more: Table 7.2 or Table 7.3? If the emphasis of the survey is on changes between groups (under 65 years vs. 65 years and older), then Table 7.2 is better. If you want to emphasize the changes that took place over a one-year period, then Table 7.3 is better.

Some Table Preparation Rules

1. Tables display columns and rows of numbers, percentages, scores, and statistical test results. Decide how many columns and rows you can include and still keep the table readable.

2. Each table should have a title that summarizes its purpose and content.

3. When the source of a table's data is not immediately obvious, it should be given.

4. When you use a term that may be confusing, define it. Set off definitions with superscript letters. Use asterisks for probability levels.

5. Columns are the independent variables such as group and timing of survey (baseline, six months later, three years later).

6. Select a table format and use it consistently. The tables in the examples here use captions in which the first letter of each main word in the columns is capitalized. In the rows, only the first word begins with a capitalized letter. Many people use only horizontal lines in tables. Use vertical lines sparingly, especially if you also use horizontal lines.

7. Present data in some logical order. One commonly used order is from most frequent to least frequent, although the reverse may be appropriate, too. This idea is to be logical so that the reader can follow.

8. Include the sample size and differentiate between numbers, percentages, and other statistics.

All word processing programs can help you format tables so that they are easy to read. If you use tables frequently, learn how to use your program's table functions.

DRAWING PIE DIAGRAMS

Pie diagrams show visually the proportion of the whole each response category occupies. Suppose you were conducting a survey of 80 library users' needs and wanted to distinguish the needs of people of different ages. Suppose also that you found that

40 respondents were relatively young, say, between 18 and 25 years of age, and only 10 were between 25 and 35 with the remaining 30 over 45 years old. You can describe your findings effectively by presenting them this way:

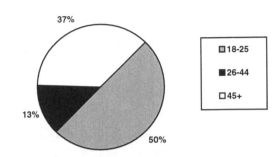

Figure 7.1. Library Users (N = 80)

Look at this:

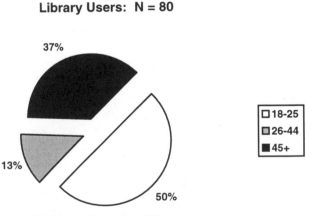

Figure 7.2. Library Users (N = 80)

This pie chart has the same proportion of users as previously. By cutting the pie, you emphasize the different sizes of each slice.

If you plan to use pie diagrams frequently, you can rely on graphics programs. All major word processing programs include graphics functions that enable you to draw pies from tables of data. The key to an accurate pie diagram is its scale. Each slice must be equal in proportion to the number or percentage of responses it represents. Fifty percent of responses is half the pie, 25% is one quarter, and so on. Remember to keep the slices to no more than about six, or the pie will be too cluttered.

USING BAR GRAPHS

Bar graphs are commonly used to display survey data because they provide an overview of several kinds of information at one glance. Look at Figure 7.3, a graph of changes in behavior between boys and girls from 1998 to 2005.

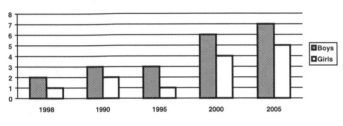

Figure 7.3. Boys' and Girls' Behavior Survey

This graph tells you two things at once:

- Boys' and girls' behavior changed over time.
- Boys had consistently higher scores than girls.

Now look at Figure 7.4. This graph of the same information concentrates on boys and girls instead of changes by year, although you still get two kinds of information at one glance.

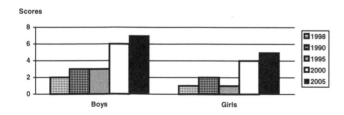

Figure 7.4. Boys' and Girls' Behavior Survey

Figure 7.5 is a graph of the same information focusing on scores, and you can see two kinds of data at once.

Bar graphs should always have a title, a legend or key to the bars, and any other explanations needed to keep the results honest. Remember that seeing can be deceiving. Just because the graph suggests differences does not mean they are real (significant and practical).

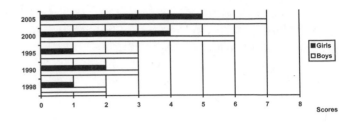

Figure 7.5. Boys' and Girls' Behavior Survey

Figure 7.6 shows the same data presented in a line graph. Line graphs are better than bars at showing the flow of change over time. Most graphics programs will allow you to automatically switch from one type of graph to another so that you can actually see which one best describes your survey data. The objective is accuracy.

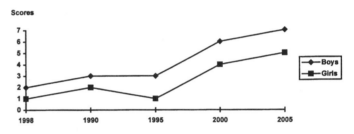

Figure 7.6. Boys' and Girls' Behavior Survey

USING LINE GRAPHS

Line graphs are drawings that allow you to show changes and compare groups. Be careful and not to oversell and make a 1-point change in score look significant unless it really is. Look at these scores:

Score	Number of Respondents With Score
1	2
2	1
3	3
4	4
5	5
6	4
Total	19

Here are two graphs, each of which has been plotted as a line graph to represent the scores and their frequency (number).

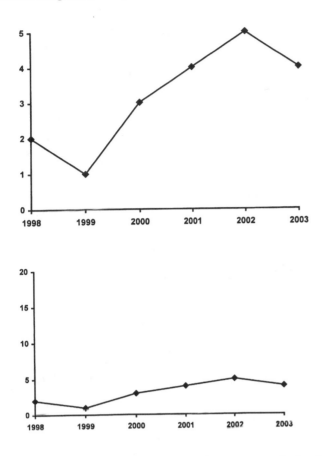

Which is more accurate? The top graph is the computer's choice. The graph below it is not. In the bottom graph, the difference in scores certainly looks less impressive.

Which is preferred, bar or line graph? If in doubt, experiment. To show comparisons, tables and bar charts seem to work best. For changes over time, line graphs win.

DRAWING DIAGRAMS OR PICTURES

Use pictures or diagrams to get your point across. Suppose you want to describe your survey's research design. Compare the words with the diagram.

Example: Words and Diagrams in Survey Reports

We used a design in which schools were the sampling units. Fourteen schools with 2,000 total students were eligible to participate in an injury prevention program. We randomly selected ten schools with a total of 945 students. Five schools with a total of 443 students were randomly assigned to receive

the curriculum, and of these students, 425 students completed the baseline survey. Of the 502 students not receiving the curriculum, 450 completed the baseline survey. We obtained 12-month follow-up data on 400 students in the five schools receiving the curriculum. One school not receiving the curriculum dropped out, and we collected 12-month follow-up survey data in the remaining four schools on 213 students.

Now look at this:

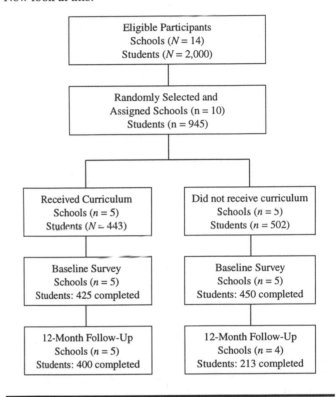

A diagram like this is very helpful in explaining complex research designs. The diagram relies on the principles that are used to make an organizational chart.

WRITING THE RESULTS OF A SURVEY

A fairly typical conclusion to a survey's activities is a written report of its purposes, methods, results, conclusions, and recommendations. One question always seems to come up when you sit down to organize the report: How detailed and technical should you be? If you are too technical you may reduce your readership substantially; on the other hand, ignoring the technical details may subject your report to criticism.

Three aims should guide your writing.

- Be comprehensive.
- Organize carefully.
- Write as clearly as you can.

Sound like one of your earliest schoolteachers warning you about a book report? Perhaps. But if these three criteria are applied, your report will be more likely to be read.

Aiming for comprehensiveness means including as much as possible so that anyone who wants to can understand the report. You must organize the report so that anyone can find out what he or she wants to know. If I am interested in why you chose the XYZ Self-Efficacy Survey, I should be able to find that information easily. Writing clearly is always a desirable aim. In survey reports, clarity means using standard language conventions and making sure that all ambiguous terms are defined.

Organizing the Report

Consider including all of these:

Abstract

Summary

Table of contents

List of tables and figures

Glossary of terms

Road map: What to look for in the report and where to find it

Statement of purposes or objectives

Outcomes

Methods

Results

Conclusions

Recommendations

References

Index

Appendix

Acknowledgments

Abstract. The abstract is usually about 200-250 words. Consider using a structured abstract. Look at this:

Example: Structured Abstract of a Survey Report

Purpose: To identify community attitudes toward integrating boys and men into Women Forward (WF), a traditionally all-female grassroots organization aimed at encouraging girls and women to enter politics.
Research design: Cross-sectional survey of 150 people
Survey: 15-minute telephone interviews conducted during July 1998
Respondents: An 82% response rate was obtained. Of the respondents, 70% were men and 62% were 35 years of age or younger. Respondents were randomly selected from local political organizations.
Main outcome: Support for integration
Results: Eighty-four men (97.6%) and 32 women (86.0%) supported integration. These differences are not significant. Respondents 35 years of age and under are significantly less eager than older respondents ($p = .04$) to integrate men into WF.
Conclusions: Although men and women are about equal in their support of integrating men into WF, younger respondents—regardless of gender—are less enthusiastic. Interpret these findings cautiously because 70% of respondents were male.

This abstract has 172 words, counting the headings. Your word processing program is likely to have a function for counting words.

Summary. The summary is a distillation of all the report's key components (objectives, methods, findings). It should be about three pages long and take five minutes to read. You can provide more detail than you do in the abstract and add information on who conducted the survey. You can also include one or two important tables or figures.

Table of Contents. The table of contents should list all major sections of the report with the associated page numbers.

List of Tables and Figures. List each table and figure and give its complete title and the page number on which it appears. In some reports, tables and figures are placed at the end in a separate section.

Glossary of Terms. All technical terms (e.g., random sampling), abbreviations (e.g., CBS = Center for Business and Science), and ambiguous concepts (e.g., healthy, smart, hostile) can be included in the glossary.

Road Map: What to Look for in the Report and Where to Find It. Some reports are complex, and the reader needs a "road map" to follow them. For instance, suppose your report has two major components: Part 1 and Part 2. Tell the reader how to find each part (Separately bound? Click on a word? An icon?). Tell what is in each (e.g., Part 1 has a description of the survey project; Part 2 discusses the validation).

Statement of Purposes or Objectives. The purposes are the survey's objectives. Discuss in the report why you did the survey. Did you do the survey to find out how satisfied participants are with their benefits? To find out which benefits will satisfy them?

Outcomes. On which main dependent variables or outcomes does the survey focus? These may be changes in knowledge, attitudes, behavior, health, or quality of life.

Methods. What was done? With whom? Was the effort worthwhile? To answer these questions, discuss:

- The type of survey (a self-administered questionnaire, telephone interview, etc.) and the limitations that resulted because you chose that type of survey. (For example, suppose that in a telephone survey of elderly persons, about 5% of eligible persons do not have access to telephones. The frailest and poorest persons will be underrepresented. Ask: What does this mean for the conclusions?)
- Survey questions asked. (Give examples; include the survey in the appendix if you cannot include it in the text.)
- Survey logistics. (During which months, over what period of time, and how frequently was the survey administered? By whom was it administered? How were the administrators trained? How was the quality of the administration monitored?) What are the limitations that resulted? (For example, say you trained five people, but one was not adequate. What might this have done to the results?)
- Survey construction. (Give the origin of questions, describe pilot testing, and discuss reliability and validity.)

Discuss the limitations that resulted during construction. (For example, the validation study may reveal that the survey is not useful with people who do not read English or Spanish at the ninth-grade level.)

- Sampling and response rate. (What were the eligibility criteria? How adequate was the response rate? Did you use incentives?) Discuss the limitations. (Because you did not get sufficient numbers of eligible respondents, what did this do to the results? For example, suppose you wanted half of the respondents to be men and half women, but respondents were primarily female?)
- Survey research design. Describe the design and its limitations. (For example, suppose your survey used comparison groups that were not randomly constituted. What types of selection bias can you anticipate? How seriously does this affect your findings?)
- Analysis. (For each main survey outcome of interest, describe the analysis method.)
- Ethics. (Were respondents informed? How was confidentiality maintained?)

Results. Concerning each outcome of interest, what did you find? Usually these are given as statistics.

Conclusions. What do the findings mean?

Recommendations. What do you recommend, based on the data? *Warning:* Not every situation warrants recommendations. Some people who commission surveys just require the data; they will themselves make the recommendations.

References. Cite those you have used in the text. Put the references in alphabetical order or list them in the order in which they appear in your text.

Index. Include an index only in very long reports.

Appendix. Include any relevant material that is too cumbersome to be contained in the report. This may mean putting a long survey into the appendix rather than the body of the report. As a rule of thumb, 15 questions or fewer can be included in the report. Keep in mind that some single questions can have 15 choices, and these might have to be put into the appendix. An example might be: In the past 12 months, have you had any one of the following health problems: headaches, stomachaches, sprained ankle or wrist, cold. Each choice is similar to a single question: In the past 12 months, have you had headaches? Have you had stomachaches? Have you had a sprained ankle or wrist? Have you had a cold?

Clear Writing

Here are some tips on clarity of items.

1. Use the active voice whenever possible.

Poor: The report is relatively simple and is obviously written for the nonexpert for there are very few statistical tables given. (Twenty words; three are forms of the verb "to be.")

Better: The relatively simple report is obviously written for the nonexpert for it gives very few statistical tables. (Seventeen words, two verbs.)

Avoid "there is" and "there are."

Poor: There are very few statistical tables in the report.

Better: The report has very few statistical tables.

2. Do not sprinkle sentences with prepositional phrases. When possible, avoid the phrase "in order to give a reason," and replace it with "to give a reason." Convert a prepositional phrase to a participle: The phrase "in the effort to get reliable attitude measures" can become "trying to get reliable attitude measures." Convert a prepositional phrase to an adjective: "It is a question of importance" can become "It is an important question."

Replace	*With*
at an early date	soon
at the present time	now
in order to	to
prior to	before
subsequent to	after

Nearly all word processing programs have a grammar function. They are excellent in pointing out the passive sentences. They also provide alternatives and can remind you of the grammar you may have forgotten. However, they are not perfect, and they are not interested in style.

3. Try a readability formula. Readability testing predicts the grade level of written material. Many people feel comfortable reading below grade level and will ignore material that is above it. Most major word processing programs will give you readability statistics for some or all of your report.

This is a simple formula that gives you a good idea of how to estimate readability. The result of using the formula is called the FOG index:

1. Take a 100-word sample of your survey report.
2. Compute the average number of words per sentence. If the final sentence in your sample runs beyond 100 words, use the total number of words at the end of that sentence to compute the average.
3. Count the number of words with more than two syllables in the 100-word sample. Do not count proper nouns or three-syllable word forms ending in *-ed* or *-es*.
4. Add the average number of words per sentence to the number of words containing more than two syllables and multiply the sum by 0.4.

Suppose a 100-word passage contains an average of 20 words per sentence and ten words of more than two syllables. The sum of these is 30. Multiplying 30 by 0.4 gives a FOG index of 12th grade.

Look at the example of the structured abstract found earlier in this chapter. The readability statistics suggest that the abstract is of average difficulty requiring a reading level from eighth to tenth grade. Most readability formulas only look at words; they do not include numbers. If you are talking to a lay audience, keep numbers simple. Use 76% or 76.2% rather than 76.17%.

THE ORAL PRESENTATION

Oral presentations follow many of the rules of written reports. Speak clearly and slowly and pace your presentation to the audience's needs. You must be selective in oral reporting, an often difficult task. Make sure you give audiences useful results. The board members want to know the bottom line; the theorists want to know about validity. Lay audiences are primarily concerned with findings and participants. If you have time, you can tell them about the survey's methods and limits. All audiences expect examples of the questions.

pants. If you have time, you can tell them about the survey's methods and limits. All audiences expect examples of the questions.

To help your presentation, consider using visual aids such as overheads and slides. Handouts and videos can enrich your presentation, but if they are not used properly, they can distract the audience. (Videos are usually too expensive to produce for the typical survey report.)

Overheads

Overheads are a relatively effective aid in oral survey reports. They are fairly inexpensive to produce, requiring a simple computer program, access to a copying machine, and special transparency paper. (If you insist, you can create overheads with special marking pens or by using 18-point or larger typewriter fonts.) Here is a sample overhead.

Example: Overhead

> ## GUIDELINES FOR PREPARING OVERHEADS
>
> - Include one main idea, table, or figure
> - Use the 6 × 6 rule
>
>   6 words per line
>
>   6 lines per overhead
> - Use simple fonts
> - Use active words
> - Use short sentences

Some additional pointers are: Do not forget to explain all tables and graphs to the audience. Make sure they understand the table's titles, its source of information, and what the numbers mean. Be careful when you use copyrighted material. You cannot automatically assume that you have permission to reproduce cartoons or anything else from a newspaper, journal, or magazine. Check that your overheads are in the correct sequence before you begin your talk.

Slides

Slides are more expensive than overheads. They are used for formal presentations. Look at this:

Example: Slides

> ## PREPARING SLIDES
>
> - Limit each slide to one concept
> - Allow 1-2 minutes per slide
> - Keep it simple: Edit tables and text
> - Use phrases (not sentences) when possible
> - Highlight key concepts: Use bold or caps
> - Discuss all information on the slide
> - Use blue background
> - Use no more than 4 colors
> - Review the slides before your talk

Computer Projection

You can project the contents of your report directly from the computer onto a screen. This technique enables you to make changes to the organization or presentation of your report based on audience suggestions. Use the same rules for preparing overheads and slides in making the presentation.

Oral reports and written reports differ in at least one very important way. Oral reports depend on

Example: Tables Used in a Written Report
and an Oral Report

Written Report

Baseline and Follow-Up Mean Scores ($\bar{x}$) and
Standard Deviations (SD)

Survey Outcome	Experimental Schools (n = 467 students)		Control Schools (n = 400 students)		Net Difference	t	p
	Baseline	Follow-Up	Baseline	Follow-Up			
Moral values	75.6 (11.8)	85.5 (8.8)	78.8 (10.9)	81.2 (9.6)	7.5	8.9	.0001
Religious beliefs	3.5 (0.7)	3.8 (0.7)	3.7 (0.7)	3.8 (0.7)	.19	4.7	.0001
Social responsibility	3.7 (0.7)	3.9 (0.7)	3.7 (0.7)	3.8 (0.7)	.10	2.2	.03
Ethical behavior	1.5 (2.5)	1.3 (2.3)	1.0 (2.0)	1.3 (2.4)	−.48	2.8	.006

NOTE: Standard deviations are in parentheses.

Interpretation. The table gives the baseline and follow-up means and the observed net differences in scores for four survey outcomes. We used an independent *t* test to compare changes in mean scores from baseline to follow-up for the experimental and control groups. Significant differences were found favoring the experimental students in moral values, religious beliefs, and social responsibility.

Oral Report

MEAN ($\bar{X}$) DIFFERENCES IN EXPERIMENTAL ($N = 467$)
AND CONTROL ($N = 400$) SCHOOLS

OUTCOME	EXPERIMENTAL $\bar{X}$		CONTROL $\bar{X}$	
	BASELINE	FOLLOW-UP	BASELINE	FOLLOW-UP
MORAL VALUES*	75.6	85.5	78.8	81.2
RELIGIOUS BELIEFS*	3.5	3.8	3.7	3.8
SOCIAL RESPONSIBILITY*	3.7	3.9	3.7	3.8
ETHICAL BEHAVIOR	1.5	1.3	1.0	1.3

*Statistically different between baseline and follow-up.

Oral Interpretation. The table compares experimental and control schools. (*Point to the appropriate columns.*) We used an independent *t* test to compare the differences in mean scores from baseline to follow-up. (*Point to the appropriate rows.*) We found statistically significant differences favoring students in experimental schools in moral values, religious beliefs, and social responsibility. (*Point to the asterisks.*)

APPENDIX

TABLE A1   Random Numbers

03 47 43 73 86	36 96 47 36 61	46 98 63 71 62	33 26 16 80 45	60 11 14 10 95
97 74 24 67 62	42 81 14 57 20	42 53 32 37 32	27 07 36 07 51	24 51 79 89 73
16 76 62 27 66	56 50 26 71 07	32 90 79 78 53	13 55 38 58 59	88 97 54 14 10
12 56 85 99 26	96 96 68 27 31	05 03 72 93 15	57 12 10 14 21	88 26 49 81 76
55 59 56 35 64	38 54 82 46 22	31 62 43 09 90	06 18 44 32 53	23 83 01 30 30
16 22 77 94 39	49 54 43 54 82	17 37 93 23 78	87 35 20 96 43	84 26 34 91 64
84 42 17 53 31	57 24 55 06 88	77 04 74 47 67	21 76 33 50 25	83 92 12 06 76
63 01 63 78 59	16 95 55 67 19	98 10 50 71 75	12 86 73 58 07	44 39 52 38 79
33 21 12 34 29	78 64 56 07 82	52 42 07 44 38	15 51 00 13 42	99 66 02 79 54
57 60 86 32 44	09 47 27 96 54	49 17 46 09 62	90 52 84 77 27	08 02 73 43 28
18 18 07 92 46	44 17 16 58 09	79 83 86 19 62	06 76 50 03 10	55 23 64 05 05
26 62 38 97 75	84 16 07 44 99	83 11 46 32 24	20 14 85 88 45	10 93 72 88 71
23 42 40 64 74	82 97 77 77 81	07 45 32 14 08	32 98 94 07 72	93 85 79 10 75
52 36 28 19 95	50 92 26 11 97	00 56 76 31 38	80 22 02 53 53	86 60 42 04 53
37 85 94 35 12	83 39 50 08 30	42 34 07 96 88	54 42 06 87 98	35 85 29 48 39
70 29 17 12 13	40 33 20 38 26	13 89 51 03 74	17 76 37 13 04	07 74 21 19 30
56 62 18 37 35	96 83 50 87 75	97 12 25 93 47	70 33 24 03 54	97 77 46 44 80
99 49 57 22 77	88 42 95 45 72	16 64 36 16 00	04 43 18 66 79	94 77 24 21 90
16 08 15 04 72	33 27 14 34 09	45 59 34 68 49	12 72 07 34 45	99 27 72 95 14
31 16 93 32 43	50 27 89 87 19	20 15 37 00 49	52 85 66 60 44	38 68 88 11 80
68 34 30 13 70	55 74 30 77 40	44 22 78 84 26	04 33 46 09 52	68 07 97 06 57
74 57 25 65 76	59 29 97 68 60	71 91 38 67 54	13 58 18 24 76	15 54 55 95 52
27 42 37 86 53	48 55 90 65 72	96 57 69 36 10	96 46 92 42 45	97 60 49 04 91
00 39 68 29 61	66 37 32 20 30	77 84 57 03 29	10 45 65 04 26	11 04 96 67 24
29 94 98 94 24	68 49 69 10 82	53 75 91 93 30	34 25 20 57 27	40 48 73 51 92
16 90 82 66 59	83 62 64 11 12	67 19 00 71 74	60 47 21 29 68	02 02 37 03 31
11 27 94 75 06	06 09 19 74 66	02 94 37 34 02	76 70 90 30 86	38 45 94 30 38
35 24 10 16 20	33 32 51 26 38	79 78 45 04 91	16 92 53 56 16	02 75 50 95 98
38 23 16 86 38	42 38 97 01 50	87 75 66 81 41	40 01 74 91 62	48 51 84 08 32
31 96 25 91 47	96 44 33 49 13	34 86 82 53 91	00 52 43 48 85	27 55 26 89 62
66 67 40 67 14	64 05 71 95 86	11 05 65 09 68	76 83 20 37 90	57 16 00 11 66
14 90 84 45 11	75 73 88 05 90	52 27 41 14 86	22 98 12 22 08	07 52 74 95 80
68 05 51 18 00	33 96 02 75 19	07 60 62 93 55	59 33 82 43 90	49 37 38 44 59
20 46 78 73 90	97 51 40 14 02	04 02 33 31 08	39 54 16 49 36	47 95 93 13 30
64 19 58 97 79	15 06 15 93 20	01 90 10 75 06	40 78 78 89 62	02 67 74 17 33
05 26 93 70 60	22 35 85 15 13	92 03 51 59 77	59 56 78 06 83	52 91 05 70 74
07 97 10 88 23	09 98 42 99 64	61 71 62 99 15	06 51 29 16 93	58 05 77 09 51
68 71 86 85 85	54 87 66 47 54	73 32 08 11 12	44 95 92 63 16	29 56 24 29 48
26 99 61 65 53	58 37 78 80 70	42 10 50 67 42	32 17 55 85 74	94 44 67 16 94
14 65 52 68 75	87 59 36 22 41	26 78 63 06 55	13 08 27 01 50	15 29 39 39 43
17 53 77 58 71	71 41 61 50 72	12 41 94 96 26	44 95 27 36 99	02 96 74 30 83
90 26 59 21 19	23 52 23 33 12	96 93 02 18 39	07 02 18 36 07	25 99 32 70 23
41 23 52 55 99	31 04 49 69 96	10 47 48 45 88	13 41 43 89 20	97 17 14 49 17
60 20 50 81 69	31 99 73 68 68	35 81 33 03 76	24 30 12 48 60	18 99 10 72 34
91 25 38 05 90	94 58 28 41 36	45 37 59 03 09	90 35 57 29 12	82 62 54 65 60
34 50 57 74 37	98 80 33 00 91	09 77 93 19 82	74 94 80 04 04	45 07 31 66 49
85 22 04 39 43	73 81 53 94 79	33 62 46 86 28	08 31 54 46 31	53 94 13 38 47
09 79 13 77 48	73 82 97 22 21	05 03 27 24 83	72 89 44 05 60	35 80 39 94 88
88 75 80 18 14	22 95 75 42 49	39 32 82 22 49	02 48 07 70 37	16 04 61 67 87
90 96 23 70 00	39 00 03 06 90	55 85 78 38 36	94 37 30 69 32	90 89 00 76 33

SOURCE: This table is taken from Table XXXIII in Fisher and Yates: *Statistical Tables for Biological, Agricultural and Medical Research,* published by Longman Group, Ltd., London (previously published by Oliver & Boyd, Ltd., Edinburgh). Used by permission of Addison Wesley Longman Ltd.

TABLE A2   Distribution of F

n_1 Degrees of Freedom (for greater mean square)

n_2^a	1	2	3	4	5	6	7	8	9	10	11	12	14	16	20	24	30	40	50	75	100	200	500	∞
1	161	200	216	225	230	234	237	239	241	242	243	245	246	246	248	249	250	251	252	253	253	254	254	254
	4,052	4,999	5,493	5,625	5,764	5,859	5,928	5,981	6,022	6,056	6,082	6,106	6,142	6,169	6,208	6,234	6,258	6,286	6,302	6,323	6,334	6,352	6,361	6,366
2	18.51	19.00	19.16	19.25	19.30	19.33	19.36	19.37	19.38	19.39	19.40	19.41	19.42	19.43	19.44	19.45	19.46	19.47	19.47	19.48	19.49	19.49	19.50	19.50
	98.49	99.00	99.17	99.25	99.30	99.33	99.34	99.36	99.38	99.40	99.41	99.42	99.43	99.44	99.45	99.46	99.47	99.48	99.48	99.49	99.49	99.49	99.50	99.50
3	10.13	9.55	9.28	9.12	9.01	8.94	8.88	8.84	8.81	8.78	8.76	8.74	8.71	8.69	8.65	8.64	8.62	8.60	8.68	8.57	8.56	8.54	8.54	8.53
	34.12	30.82	29.46	28.71	28.24	27.91	27.67	27.49	27.34	27.23	27.13	27.05	26.92	26.83	26.69	26.60	26.50	26.41	26.35	26.27	26.23	26.18	26.14	26.12
4	7.71	6.94	6.69	6.39	6.26	6.16	6.09	6.04	6.00	5.96	5.93	5.91	5.87	5.84	5.80	5.77	5.74	5.71	5.70	5.68	5.66	5.65	5.64	5.63
	21.20	18.00	16.69	15.98	15.52	15.21	14.98	14.80	14.66	14.54	14.45	14.37	14.24	14.15	14.02	13.93	13.83	13.74	13.69	13.61	13.57	13.52	13.48	13.46
5	6.61	5.79	5.41	5.19	5.05	4.95	4.88	4.82	4.78	4.74	4.70	4.68	4.64	4.60	4.56	4.53	4.50	4.46	4.44	4.42	4.40	4.38	4.37	4.36
	16.26	13.27	12.06	11.39	10.97	10.67	10.45	10.27	10.15	10.05	9.96	9.89	9.77	9.68	9.55	9.47	9.38	9.29	9.24	9.17	9.13	9.07	9.04	9.02
6	5.99	5.14	4.76	4.53	4.39	4.28	4.21	4.15	4.10	4.06	4.03	4.00	3.96	3.92	3.87	3.84	3.81	3.77	3.75	3.72	3.71	3.69	3.68	3.67
	13.74	10.92	9.78	9.15	8.75	8.47	8.26	8.19	7.98	7.87	7.79	7.72	7.60	7.52	7.39	7.31	7.23	7.14	7.09	7.02	6.99	6.94	6.90	6.88
7	5.59	4.74	4.35	4.12	3.97	3.87	3.79	3.73	3.68	3.63	3.60	3.57	3.52	3.49	3.44	3.41	3.38	3.34	3.32	3.29	3.28	3.25	3.24	3.23
	12.25	9.55	8.45	7.85	7.46	7.19	7.00	6.84	6.71	6.62	6.54	6.47	6.35	6.27	6.15	6.07	5.98	5.90	5.85	5.78	5.75	5.70	5.67	5.65
8	5.32	4.46	4.07	3.84	3.69	3.58	3.50	3.44	3.39	3.34	3.31	3.28	3.23	3.20	3.15	3.12	3.08	3.05	3.03	3.00	2.98	2.96	2.94	2.93
	11.26	8.65	7.59	7.61	6.63	6.37	6.19	6.03	5.91	5.82	5.74	5.67	5.56	5.48	5.36	5.28	5.20	5.11	5.06	5.00	4.96	4.91	4.88	4.86
9	5.12	4.26	3.86	3.63	3.48	3.37	3.29	3.23	3.18	3.13	3.10	3.07	3.02	2.98	2.93	2.90	2.86	2.82	2.80	2.77	2.76	2.73	2.72	2.71
	10.56	8.02	6.99	6.42	6.06	5.80	5.62	5.47	5.35	5.26	5.18	5.11	5.00	4.92	4.80	4.73	4.64	4.56	4.51	4.45	4.41	4.36	4.33	4.31
10	4.96	4.10	3.71	3.48	3.33	3.22	3.14	3.07	3.02	2.97	2.94	2.91	2.86	2.82	2.77	2.74	2.70	2.67	2.64	2.61	2.59	2.56	2.55	2.54
	10.04	7.56	6.55	5.99	5.64	5.39	5.21	5.06	4.95	4.85	4.78	4.71	4.60	4.52	4.41	4.33	4.25	4.17	4.12	4.05	4.01	3.96	3.93	3.91
11	4.84	3.98	3.59	3.36	3.20	3.09	3.01	2.95	2.90	2.86	2.82	2.79	2.74	2.70	2.65	2.61	2.57	2.53	2.50	2.47	2.45	2.42	2.41	2.40
	9.65	7.20	6.22	5.67	5.32	5.07	4.88	4.74	4.63	4.54	4.46	4.40	4.29	4.21	4.10	4.02	3.94	3.86	3.80	3.74	3.70	3.66	3.62	3.60
12	4.75	3.88	3.49	3.26	3.11	3.00	2.92	2.85	2.80	2.76	2.72	2.69	2.64	2.60	2.54	2.50	2.46	2.42	2.40	2.36	2.35	2.32	2.31	2.30
	9.33	6.93	5.95	8.41	5.06	4.82	4.65	4.50	4.39	4.30	4.22	4.16	4.05	3.98	3.86	3.78	3.70	3.61	3.56	3.49	3.46	3.41	3.38	3.36
13	4.67	3.80	3.41	3.18	3.02	2.92	2.84	2.77	2.72	2.67	2.63	2.60	2.55	2.51	2.46	2.42	2.38	2.34	2.32	2.28	2.26	2.24	2.22	2.21
	9.07	6.70	5.74	5.20	4.86	4.62	4.44	4.30	4.19	4.10	4.02	3.96	3.85	3.78	3.67	3.59	3.51	3.42	3.37	3.30	3.27	3.21	3.18	3.16
14	4.00	3.74	3.34	3.11	2.96	2.85	2.77	2.70	2.65	2.60	2.56	2.53	2.48	2.44	2.39	2.35	2.31	2.27	2.24	2.21	2.19	2.16	2.14	2.13
	8.56	6.51	5.56	5.03	4.69	4.46	4.28	4.14	4.03	3.94	3.86	3.80	3.70	3.62	3.51	3.43	3.34	3.26	3.21	3.14	3.11	3.06	3.02	3.00
15	4.54	3.68	3.29	3.06	2.90	2.79	2.70	2.64	2.59	2.55	2.51	2.48	2.43	2.39	2.33	2.29	2.25	2.21	2.18	2.15	2.12	2.10	2.08	2.07
	8.68	6.36	5.42	4.89	4.56	4.32	4.14	4.00	3.89	3.80	3.73	3.67	3.56	3.48	3.36	3.29	3.20	3.12	3.07	3.00	2.97	2.92	2.89	2.87
16	4.49	3.63	3.24	3.01	2.85	2.74	2.66	2.59	2.54	2.49	2.45	2.42	2.37	2.33	2.28	2.24	2.20	2.16	2.13	2.09	2.07	2.04	2.02	2.01
	8.53	6.23	5.29	4.77	4.44	4.20	4.03	3.89	3.78	3.69	3.61	3.55	3.45	3.37	3.25	3.18	3.10	3.01	2.96	2.89	2.86	2.80	2.77	2.75
17	4.45	3.59	3.20	2.96	2.81	2.70	2.62	2.55	2.50	2.45	2.41	2.38	2.33	2.29	2.23	2.19	2.15	2.11	2.08	2.04	2.02	1.99	1.97	1.96
	8.40	6.11	5.18	4.67	4.34	4.10	3.93	3.79	3.68	3.59	3.52	3.45	3.35	3.27	3.16	3.08	3.00	2.92	2.86	2.79	2.76	2.70	2.67	2.65
18	4.41	3.55	3.16	2.93	2.77	2.66	2.58	2.51	2.46	2.41	2.37	2.34	2.29	2.25	2.19	2.15	2.11	2.07	2.04	2.00	1.98	1.95	1.93	1.92
	8.28	6.01	5.09	4.58	4.25	4.01	3.85	3.71	3.60	3.51	3.44	3.37	3.27	3.19	3.07	3.00	2.91	2.83	2.78	2.71	2.68	2.62	2.59	2.57
19	4.38	3.52	3.13	2.90	2.74	2.63	2.55	2.48	2.43	2.38	2.34	2.31	2.26	2.21	2.15	2.11	2.07	2.02	2.00	1.96	1.94	1.91	1.90	1.88
	8.18	5.93	5.01	4.50	4.17	3.94	3.77	3.63	3.52	3.43	3.36	3.30	3.19	3.12	3.00	2.92	2.84	2.76	2.70	2.63	2.60	2.54	2.51	2.49
20	4.35	3.49	3.10	2.87	2.71	2.60	2.52	2.45	2.40	2.35	2.31	2.28	2.23	2.18	2.12	2.08	2.04	1.99	1.96	1.92	1.90	1.87	1.85	1.84
	8.10	5.85	4.94	4.43	4.10	3.87	3.71	3.56	3.45	3.37	3.30	3.23	3.13	3.05	2.94	2.86	2.77	2.69	2.63	2.56	2.53	2.47	2.44	2.42
21	4.32	3.47	3.07	2.84	2.68	2.57	2.49	2.42	2.37	2.32	2.28	2.25	2.20	2.15	2.09	2.05	2.00	1.96	1.93	1.89	1.87	1.84	1.82	1.81
	8.02	5.78	4.87	4.37	4.04	3.81	3.65	3.51	3.40	3.31	3.24	3.17	3.07	2.99	2.88	2.80	2.72	2.63	2.58	2.51	2.47	2.42	2.38	2.36
22	4.30	3.44	3.05	2.82	2.66	2.65	2.47	2.40	2.35	2.30	2.26	2.23	2.18	2.13	2.07	2.03	1.98	1.93	1.91	1.87	1.84	1.81	1.80	1.78
	7.94	5.72	4.82	4.31	3.99	3.76	3.59	3.45	3.35	3.26	3.18	3.12	3.02	2.94	2.83	2.75	2.67	2.58	2.53	2.46	2.42	2.37	2.33	2.31
23	4.28	3.42	3.03	2.80	2.64	2.53	2.45	2.38	2.32	2.28	2.24	2.20	2.14	2.10	2.04	2.00	1.96	1.91	1.88	1.84	1.82	1.79	1.77	1.76
	7.88	5.66	4.76	4.26	3.94	3.71	3.54	3.41	3.30	3.21	3.14	3.07	2.97	2.89	2.78	2.70	2.62	2.53	2.48	2.41	2.37	2.32	2.28	2.26
24	4.26	3.40	3.01	2.78	2.62	2.51	2.43	2.36	2.30	2.26	2.22	2.18	2.13	2.09	2.02	1.98	1.94	1.89	1.86	1.82	1.80	1.76	1.74	1.73
	7.82	5.61	4.72	4.22	3.90	3.67	3.50	3.36	3.25	3.17	3.09	3.03	2.93	2.85	2.74	2.66	2.58	2.49	2.44	2.36	2.33	2.27	2.23	2.21
25	4.24	3.38	2.99	2.76	2.60	2.49	2.41	2.34	2.28	2.24	2.20	2.16	2.11	2.06	2.00	1.96	1.92	1.87	1.84	1.80	1.77	1.74	1.72	1.71
	7.77	5.57	4.68	4.18	3.86	3.63	3.46	3.32	3.21	3.13	3.05	2.99	2.89	2.81	2.70	2.62	2.54	2.45	2.40	2.32	2.29	2.23	2.19	2.17
26	4.22	3.37	2.98	2.74	2.59	2.47	2.39	2.32	2.27	2.22	2.18	2.15	2.10	2.05	1.99	1.95	1.90	1.85	1.82	1.78	1.76	1.72	1.70	1.69
	7.72	5.53	4.64	4.14	3.82	3.59	3.42	3.29	3.17	3.09	3.02	2.96	2.86	2.77	2.66	2.58	2.50	2.41	2.36	2.28	2.25	2.19	2.15	2.13
27	4.21	3.35	2.96	2.73	2.57	2.46	2.37	2.30	2.25	2.20	2.16	2.13	2.08	2.03	1.97	1.93	1.88	1.84	1.80	1.76	1.74	1.71	1.68	1.67
	7.68	5.49	4.60	4.11	3.79	3.56	3.39	3.26	3.14	3.06	2.98	2.93	2.83	2.74	2.63	2.55	2.47	2.38	2.33	2.25	2.21	2.16	2.12	2.18

TABLE A2 Continued

n_1 Degrees of Freedom (for greater mean square)

$n_2{}^a$	1	2	3	4	5	6	7	8	9	10	11	12	14	16	20	24	30	40	50	75	100	200	500	∞
28	4.20	3.34	2.95	2.71	2.56	2.44	2.36	2.29	2.24	2.19	2.15	2.12	2.06	2.02	1.96	1.91	1.87	1.81	1.78	1.75	1.72	1.69	1.67	1.65
	7.64	5.45	4.57	4.07	3.76	3.53	3.36	3.23	3.11	3.03	2.95	2.90	2.80	2.71	2.68	2.52	2.44	2.35	2.30	2.22	2.18	2.13	2.89	2.86
29	4.18	3.33	2.93	2.70	2.54	2.43	2.35	2.28	2.22	2.18	2.14	2.10	2.05	2.00	1.94	1.90	1.85	1.80	1.77	1.73	1.71	1.68	1.65	1.64
	7.60	5.42	4.54	4.04	3.73	3.50	3.33	3.20	3.08	3.00	2.92	2.87	2.77	2.68	2.57	2.49	2.41	2.32	2.27	2.19	2.15	2.10	2.06	2.03
30	4.17	3.32	2.92	2.69	2.53	2.42	2.34	2.27	2.21	2.16	2.12	2.09	2.04	1.99	1.93	1.89	1.84	1.79	1.76	1.72	1.69	1.66	1.64	1.62
	7.56	5.39	4.51	4.02	3.70	3.47	3.30	3.17	3.06	2.98	2.90	2.84	2.74	2.66	2.55	2.47	2.38	2.29	2.24	2.16	2.13	2.07	2.03	2.01
32	4.15	3.30	2.90	2.67	2.51	2.40	2.32	2.25	2.19	2.14	2.10	2.07	2.02	1.97	1.91	1.86	1.82	1.75	1.74	1.69	1.67	1.64	1.61	1.69
	7.50	5.34	4.46	3.97	3.66	3.42	3.25	3.12	3.81	2.94	2.86	2.80	2.70	2.62	2.51	2.42	2.34	2.25	2.20	2.12	2.08	2.02	1.98	1.96
34	4.13	3.28	2.88	2.65	2.49	2.38	2.30	2.23	2.17	2.12	2.08	2.05	2.00	195	1.89	1.84	1.80	1.74	1.71	1.67	1.64	1.61	1.59	1.57
	7.44	5.29	4.42	3.93	3.61	3.38	3.21	3.08	2.97	2.89	2.82	2.76	2.66	2.58	2.47	2.38	2.30	2.21	2.15	2.08	2.04	1.98	1.94	1.91
36	4.11	3.26	2.86	2.63	2.48	2.36	2.28	2.21	2.15	2.10	2.06	2.03	1.98	1.93	1.87	1.82	1.78	1.72	1.69	1.65	1.62	1.59	1.56	1.55
	7.39	5.25	4.38	3.89	3.58	3.35	3.18	3.04	2.94	2.86	2.78	2.72	2.62	2.54	2.43	2.35	2.26	2.17	2.12	2.04	2.00	1.94	1.90	1.87
38	4.10	3.25	2.85	2.62	2.46	2.35	2.26	2.19	2.14	2.09	2.05	2.02	1.96	1.92	1.85	1.80	1.76	1.71	1.67	1.63	1.60	1.57	1.54	1.53
	7.35	5.21	4.34	3.86	3.54	3.32	3.15	3.02	2.91	2.82	2.75	2.69	2.59	2.51	2.40	2.32	2.22	2.14	2.08	2.00	1.97	1.90	1.86	1.84
40	4.08	3.23	2.84	2.61	2.45	2.34	2.25	2.18	2.12	2.07	2.04	2.00	1.95	1.90	1.84	1.79	1.74	1.69	1.66	1.61	1.59	1.55	1.53	1.51
	7.31	5.18	4.31	3.83	3.51	3.29	3.12	2.99	2.88	2.80	2.73	2.66	2.56	2.49	2.37	2.29	2.20	2.11	2.05	1.97	1.94	1.88	1.84	1.81
42	4.07	3.22	2.83	2.59	2.44	2.32	2.24	2.17	2.11	2.06	2.02	1.99	1.94	1.89	1.82	1.78	1.73	1.68	1.64	1.60	1.57	1.54	1.51	1.49
	7.27	5.15	4.29	3.80	3.49	3.26	3.18	2.96	2.86	2.77	2.70	2.64	2.54	2.46	2.35	2.26	2.17	2.08	2.02	1.94	1.91	1.85	1.80	1.78
44	4.06	3.21	2.82	2.58	2.43	2.31	2.23	2.16	2.10	2.05	2.01	1.98	1.92	1.88	1.81	1.76	1.72	1.66	1.63	1.58	1.56	1.52	1.50	1.48
	7.24	5.12	4.26	3.78	3.46	3.24	3.07	2.94	2.84	2.75	2.68	2.62	2.52	2.44	2.32	2.24	2.15	2.06	2.00	1.92	1.88	1.82	1.78	1.75
46	4.05	3.20	2.81	2.57	2.42	2.30	2.22	2.14	2.09	2.04	2.00	1.97	1.91	1.87	1.80	1.75	1.71	1.65	1.62	1.57	1.54	1.51	1.48	1.46
	7.21	5.10	4.24	3.76	3.44	3.22	3.05	2.92	2.82	2.73	2.66	2.60	2.50	2.42	2.30	2.22	2.13	2.04	1.98	1.90	1.86	1.80	1.76	1.72
48	4.04	3.19	2.80	2.56	2.41	2.30	2.21	2.14	2.08	2.03	1.99	1.96	1.90	1.86	1.79	1.74	1.70	1.64	1.61	1.56	1.53	1.50	1.47	1.45
	7.19	5.08	4.22	3.74	3.42	3.20	3.04	2.90	2.80	2.71	2.64	2.58	2.48	2.40	2.28	2.20	2.11	2.02	1.96	1.88	1.84	1.78	1.73	1.70
50	4.03	3.18	2.79	2.56	2.40	2.29	2.20	2.13	2.07	2.02	1.98	1.95	1.90	1.85	1.78	1.74	1.69	1.63	1.60	1.55	1.52	1.48	1.46	1.44
	7.17	5.06	4.20	3.72	3.41	3.18	3.02	2.88	2.78	2.70	2.62	2.56	2.46	2.39	2.26	2.18	2.10	2.00	1.94	1.86	1.82	1.76	1.71	1.68
55	4.02	3.17	2.78	2.54	2.38	2.27	2.18	2.11	2.05	2.00	1.97	1.93	1.88	1.83	1.76	1.72	1.67	1.61	1.58	1.52	1.50	1.46	1.43	1.41
	7.12	5.01	4.16	3.68	3.37	3.15	2.98	2.85	2.75	2.66	2.59	2.53	2.43	2.35	2.23	2.15	2.06	1.96	1.90	1.82	1.78	1.71	1.66	1.64
60	4.00	3.15	2.76	2.52	2.37	2.25	2.17	2.10	2.04	1.99	1.95	1.92	1.86	1.81	1.75	1.70	1.65	1.69	1.55	1.50	1.48	1.44	1.41	1.39
	7.08	4.98	4.13	3.65	3.34	3.12	2.95	2.82	2.72	2.63	2.56	2.50	2.40	2.32	2.20	2.12	2.03	1.93	1.87	1.79	1.74	1.68	1.63	1.60
65	3.99	3.14	2.75	2.51	2.36	2.24	2.15	2.08	2.02	1.98	1.94	1.90	1.85	1.80	1.73	1.68	1.63	1.57	1.54	1.49	1.46	1.42	1.39	1.37
	7.04	4.95	4.10	3.62	3.31	3.09	2.93	2.79	2.70	2.61	2.54	2.47	2.37	2.30	2.18	2.09	2.00	1.90	1.84	1.76	1.71	1.64	1.60	1.56
70	3.98	3.13	2.74	2.50	2.35	2.23	2.14	2.07	2.01	1.97	1.93	1.89	1.84	1.79	1.72	1.67	1.62	1.56	1.53	1.47	1.45	1.40	1.37	1.35
	7.01	4.92	4.08	3.60	3.29	3.07	2.91	2.77	2.67	2.59	2.51	2.45	2.35	2.28	2.15	2.07	1.98	1.88	1.82	1.74	1.69	1.62	1.56	1.53
80	3.96	3.11	2.72	2.48	2.33	2.21	2.12	2.05	1.99	1.95	1.91	1.88	1.82	1.77	1.70	1.65	1.60	1.54	1.51	1.45	1.42	1.38	1.35	1.32
	6.96	4.88	4.84	3.56	3.25	3.04	2.87	2.74	2.64	2.55	2.48	2.41	2.32	2.24	2.11	2.03	1.94	1.84	1.78	1.70	1.65	1.57	1.52	1.49
100	3.94	3.09	2.70	2.46	2.30	2.19	2.10	2.03	1.97	1.92	1.88	1.85	1.79	1.75	1.68	1.63	1.57	1.51	1.48	1.42	1.39	1.34	1.30	1.28
	6.90	4.82	3.98	3.51	3.20	2.99	2.82	2.69	2.59	2.51	2.43	2.36	2.26	2.19	2.06	1.98	1.89	1.79	1.73	1.64	1.59	1.51	1.46	1.43
125	3.92	3.07	2.68	2.44	2.29	2.17	2.08	2.01	1.95	1.90	1.86	1.83	1.77	1.72	1.65	1.60	1.55	1.49	1.45	1.39	1.36	1.31	1.27	1.25
	6.84	4.78	3.94	3.47	3.17	2.95	2.79	2.65	2.56	2.47	2.40	2.33	2.23	2.15	2.03	1.94	1.85	1.75	1.68	1.59	1.54	1.46	1.40	1.37
150	3.91	3.06	2.67	2.43	2.27	2.16	2.07	2.00	1.94	1.89	1.85	1.82	1.76	1.71	1.64	1.69	1.54	1.47	1.44	1.37	1.34	1.29	1.25	1.22
	6.81	4.75	3.91	3.44	3.14	2.92	2.76	2.62	2.53	2.44	2.37	2.30	2.20	2.12	2.00	1.91	1.83	1.72	1.66	1.56	1.51	1.43	1.37	1.33
200	3.89	3.04	2.65	2.41	2.26	2.14	2.05	1.98	1.92	1.87	1.83	1.80	1.74	1.69	1.62	1.57	1.52	1.45	1.42	1.35	1.32	1.26	1.22	1.19
	6.76	4.71	3.88	3.41	3.11	2.90	2.73	2.68	2.50	2.41	2.34	2.28	2.17	2.09	1.97	1.88	1.79	1.69	1.62	1.53	1.48	1.39	1.33	1.28
400	3.86	3.02	2.62	2.39	2.23	2.12	2.03	1.96	1.90	1.85	1.81	1.78	1.72	1.67	1.60	1.54	1.49	1.42	1.38	1.32	1.28	1.22	1.16	1.13
	6.70	4.66	3.83	3.36	3.06	2.85	2.69	2.55	2.46	2.37	2.29	2.23	2.12	2.04	1.92	1.84	1.74	1.64	1.57	1.47	1.42	1.32	1.24	1.19
1,000	3.85	3.00	2.61	2.38	2.22	2.10	2.02	1.95	1.89	1.84	1.80	1.76	1.70	1.65	1.58	1.53	1.47	1.41	1.36	1.30	1.23	1.19	1.13	1.08
	6.66	4.62	3.88	3.34	3.04	2.82	2.66	2.53	2.43	2.34	2.26	2.20	2.09	2.01	1.89	1.81	1.71	1.61	1.54	1.44	1.38	1.28	1.19	1.11
∞	3.84	2.99	2.60	2.37	2.21	2.09	2.01	1.94	1.88	1.83	1.79	1.75	1.69	1.64	1.57	1.52	1.46	1.40	1.35	1.28	1.24	1.17	1.11	1.00
	6.64	4.60	3.78	3.32	3.81	2.88	2.64	2.51	2.41	2.32	2.24	2.18	2.07	1.99	1.87	1.79	1.69	1.59	1.52	1.41	1.36	1.25	1.15	1.00

SOURCE: Reprinted by permission from *Statistical Methods* by George W. Snedecor and William G. Cochran. © 1980 by the Iowa State University Press, Ames, Iowa 50010. Used with permission.
NOTE: The function $F = e$ with exponent $2z$ is computed in part from Fisher's table VI(7). Additional entries are by interpolation, mostly graphical.
a. n_2 = degrees of freedom for the lesser mean squared.

TABLE A3 Distribution of *t*

	Probability													
n^a	.9	.8	.7	.6	.5	.4	.3	.2	.1	.05	.02	.01	.001
1	.158	.325	.510	.727	1.000	1.376	1.963	3.078	6.314	12.706	31.821	63.657	636.619
2	.142	.289	.445	.617	.816	1.061	1.386	1.886	2.920	4.303	6.965	9.925	31.598
3	.137	.277	.424	.584	.765	.978	1.250	1.638	2.353	3.182	4.541	5.841	12.924
4	.134	.271	.414	569	.741	.941	1.190	1.533	2.132	2.776	3.747	4.604	8.610
5	.132	.267	.408	.559	.727	.920	1.156	1.476	2.015	2.571	3.365	4.032	6.869
6	.131	.265	.404	.553	.718	.906	1.134	1.440	1.943	2.447	3.143	3.707	5.959
7	.130	.263	.402	.549	.711	.896	1.119	1.415	1.895	2.365	2.998	3.499	5.408
8	.130	.262	.399	.546	.706	.889	1.108	1.397	1.860	2.306	2.896	3.355	5.041
9	.129	.261	.398	.543	.703	.883	1.100	1.383	1.833	2.262	2.821	3.250	4.781
10	.129	.260	.397	.542	.700	.879	1.093	1.372	1.812	2.228	2.764	3.169	4.587
11	.129	.260	.396	.540	.697	.876	1.088	1.363	1.796	2.201	2.718	3.106	4.437
12	.128	.259	.395	.539	.695	.873	1.083	1.356	1.782	2.179	2.681	3.055	4.318
13	.128	.259	.394	.538	.694	.870	1.079	1.350	1.771	2.160	2.650	3.012	4.221
14	.128	.258	.393	.537	.692	.868	1.076	1.345	1.761	2.145	2.624	2.977	4.140
15	.128	.258	.393	.536	.691	.866	1.074	1.341	1.753	2.131	2.602	2.947	4.073
16	.128	.258	.392	.535	.690	.865	1.071	1.337	1.746	2.120	2.583	2.921	4.015
17	.128	.257	.392	.534	.689	.863	1.069	1.333	1.740	2.110	2.567	2.898	3.965
18	.127	.257	.392	.534	.688	.862	1.067	1.330	1.734	2.101	2.552	2.878	3.922
19	.127	.257	.391	.533	.688	.861	1.066	1.328	1.729	2.093	2.539	2.861	3.883
20	.127	.257	.391	.533	.687	.860	1.064	1.325	1.725	2.086	2.528	2.845	3.850
21	.127	.257	.391	.532	.686	.859	1.063	1.323	1.721	2.080	2.518	2.831	3.819
22	.127	.256	.390	.532	.686	.858	1.061	1.321	1.717	2.074	2.508	2.819	3.792
23	.127	.256	.390	.532	.685	.858	1.060	1.319	1.714	2.069	2.500	2.807	3.767
24	.127	.256	.390	.531	.685	.857	1.059	1.318	1.711	2.064	2.492	2.797	3.745
25	.127	.256	.390	.531	.684	.856	1.058	1.316	1.708	2.060	2.485	2.787	3.725
26	.127	.256	.390	.531	.684	.856	1.058	1.315	1.706	2.056	2.479	2.779	3.707
27	.127	.256	.389	.531	.684	.855	1.057	1.314	1.703	2.052	2.473	2.771	3.690
28	.127	.256	.389	.530	.683	.855	1.056	1.313	1.701	2.048	2.467	2.763	3.674
29	.127	.256	.389	.530	.683	.854	1.055	1.311	1.699	2.045	2.462	2.756	3.659
30	.127	.256	.389	.530	.683	.854	1.055	1.310	1.697	2.042	2.457	2.750	3.646
40	.126	.255	.388	.529	.681	.851	1.050	1.303	1.684	2.021	2.423	2.704	3.551
60	.126	.254	.387	.527	.679	.848	1.046	1.296	1.671	2.000	2.390	2.660	3.460
120	.126	.254	.386	.526	.677	.845	1.041	1.289	1.658	1.980	2.358	2.617	3.373
∞	.126	.253	.385	.524	.674	.842	1.036	1.282	1.645	1.960	2.326	2.576	3.291

SOURCE: This table is taken from Table III in Fisher and Yates: *Statistical Tables for Biological, Agricultural and Medical Research,* published by Longman Group, Ltd., London (previously published by Oliver & Boyd, Ltd., Edinburgh). Used by permission of Addison Wesley Longman Ltd.
a. *n* = degrees of freedom.

TABLE A4   Distribution of χ^2

n^{a}	Probability													
	.99	.98	.95	.90	.80	.70	.50	.30	.20	.10	.05	.02	.01	.001
1	.03157	.03628	.00393	.0158	.0642	.148	.455	1.074	1.642	2.706	3.841	5.412	6.635	10.827
2	.0201	.0404	.103	.211	.446	.713	1.386	2.408	3.219	4.605	5.991	7.824	9.210	13.815
3	.115	.185	.352	.584	1.005	1.424	2.366	3.665	4.642	6.251	7.815	9.837	11.345	16.266
4	.297	.429	.711	1.064	1.649	2.195	3.357	4.878	5.989	7.779	9.488	11.668	13.277	18.467
5	.554	.752	1.145	1.610	2.343	3.000	4.351	6.064	7.289	9.236	11.070	13.388	15.086	20.515
6	.872	1.134	1.635	2.204	3.070	3.828	5.348	7.231	8.558	10.645	12.592	15.033	16.812	22.457
7	1.239	1.564	2.167	2.833	3.822	4.671	6.346	8.383	9.803	12.017	14.067	16.622	18.475	24.322
8	1.646	2.032	2.733	3.490	4.594	5.527	7.344	9.524	11.030	13.362	15.507	18.168	20.090	26.125
9	2.088	2.532	3.325	4.168	5.380	6.393	8.343	10.656	12.242	14.684	16.919	19.679	21.666	27.877
10	2.558	3.059	3.940	4.865	6.179	7.267	9.342	11.781	13.442	15.987	18.307	21.161	23.209	29.588
11	3.053	3.609	4.575	5.578	6.989	8.148	10.341	12.899	14.631	17.275	19.675	22.618	24.725	31.264
12	3.571	4.178	5.226	6.304	7.807	9.034	11.340	14.011	15.812	18.549	21.026	24.054	26.217	32.909
13	4.107	4.765	5.892	7.042	8.634	9.926	12.340	15.119	16.985	19.812	22.362	25.472	27.688	34.528
14	4.660	5.368	6.571	7.790	9.467	10.821	13.339	16.222	18.151	21.064	23.685	26.873	29.141	36.123
15	5.229	5.985	7.261	8.547	10.307	11.721	14.339	17.322	19.311	22.307	24.996	28.259	30.578	37.697
16	5.812	6.614	7.962	9.312	11.152	12.624	15.338	18.418	20.465	23.542	26.296	29.633	32.000	39.252
17	6.408	7.255	8.672	10.085	12.002	13.531	16.338	19.511	21.615	24.769	27.587	30.995	33.409	40.790
18	7.015	7.906	9.390	10.865	12.857	14.440	17.338	20.601	22.760	25.989	28.869	32.346	34.805	42.312
19	7.633	8.567	10.117	11.651	13.716	15.352	18.338	21.689	23.900	27.204	30.144	33.687	36.191	43.820
20	8.260	9.237	10.851	12.443	14.578	16.266	19.337	22.775	25.038	28.412	31.410	35.020	37.566	45.315
21	8.897	9.915	11.591	13.240	15.445	17.182	20.337	23.858	26.171	29.615	32.671	36.343	38.932	46.797
22	9.542	10.600	12.338	14.041	16.314	18.101	21.337	24.939	27.301	30.813	33.924	37.659	40.289	48.268
23	10.196	11.293	13.091	14.848	17.187	19.021	22.337	26.018	28.429	32.007	35.172	38.968	41.638	49.728
24	10.856	11.992	13.848	15.659	18.062	19.943	23.337	27.096	29.553	33.196	36.415	40.270	42.980	51.179
25	11.524	12.697	14.611	16.473	18.940	20.867	24.337	28.172	30.675	34.382	37.652	41.566	44.314	52.620
26	12.198	13.409	15.379	17.292	19.820	21.792	25.336	29.246	31.795	35.563	38.885	42.856	45.642	54.052
27	12.879	14.125	16.151	18.114	20.703	22.719	26.336	30.319	32.912	36.741	40.113	44.140	46.963	55.476
28	13.565	14.847	16.928	18.939	21.588	23.647	27.336	31.391	34.027	37.916	41.337	45.419	48.278	56.893
29	14.256	15.574	17.708	19.768	22.475	24.577	28.336	32.461	35.139	39.087	42.557	46.693	49.588	58.302
30	14.953	16.306	18.493	20.599	23.364	25.508	29.336	33.530	36.250	40.256	43.773	47.962	50.892	59.703
32	16.362	17.783	20.072	22.271	25.148	27.373	31.336	35.665	38.466	42.585	46.194	50.487	53.486	62.487
34	17.789	19.275	21.664	23.952	26.938	29.242	33.336	37.795	40.676	44.903	48.602	52.995	56.061	65.247
36	19.233	20.783	23.269	25.643	28.735	31.115	35.336	39.922	42.879	47.212	50.999	55.489	58.619	67.985
38	20.691	22.304	24.884	27.343	30.537	32.992	37.335	42.045	45.076	49.513	53.384	57.969	61.162	70.703
40	22.164	23.838	26.509	29.051	32.345	34.872	39.335	44.165	47.269	51.805	55.759	60.436	63.691	73.402
42	23.650	25.383	28.144	30.765	34.157	36.755	41.335	46.282	49.456	54.090	58.124	62.892	66.206	76.084
44	25.148	26.939	29.787	32.487	35.974	38.641	43.335	48.396	51.639	56.369	60.481	65.337	68.710	78.750
46	26.657	28.504	31.439	34.215	37.795	40.529	45.335	50.507	53.818	58.641	62.830	67.771	71.201	81.400
48	28.177	30.080	33.098	35.949	39.621	42.420	47.335	52.616	55.993	60.907	65.171	70.197	73.683	84.037
50	29.707	31.664	34.764	37.689	41.449	44.313	49.335	54.723	58.164	63.167	67.505	72.613	76.154	86.661
52	31.246	33.256	36.437	39.433	43.281	46.209	51.335	56.827	60.332	65.422	69.832	75.021	78.616	89.272
54	32.793	34.856	38.116	41.183	45.117	48.106	53.335	58.930	62.496	67.673	72.153	77.422	81.069	91.872
56	34.350	36.464	39.801	42.937	46.955	50.005	55.335	61.031	64.658	69.919	74.468	79.815	83.513	94.461
58	35.913	38.078	41.492	44.696	48.797	51.906	57.335	63.129	66.816	72.160	76.778	82.201	85.950	97.039
60	37.485	39.699	43.188	46.459	50.641	53.809	59.335	65.227	68.972	74.397	79.082	84.580	88.379	99.607
62	39.063	41.327	44.889	48.226	52.487	55.714	61.335	67.322	71.125	76.630	81.381	86.953	90.802	102.166
64	40.649	42.960	46.595	49.996	34.336	57.620	63.335	69.416	73.276	78.860	83.675	89.320	93.217	104.716
66	42.240	44.599	48.305	51.770	56.188	59.527	65.335	71.508	75.424	81.085	85.965	91.681	95.626	107.258
68	43.838	46.244	50.020	53.548	58.042	61.436	67.335	73.600	77.571	83.308	88.250	94.037	98.028	109.791
70	45.442	47.893	51.739	55.329	59.898	63.346	69.334	75.689	79.715	85.527	90.531	96.388	100.425	112.317

SOURCE: This table is taken from Table IV in Fisher and Yates: *Statistical Tables for Biological, Agricultural and Medical Research,* published by Longman Group, Ltd., London (previously published by Oliver & Boyd, Ltd., Edinburgh). Used by permission of Addison Wesley Longman Ltd.

NOTE: For odd values of n between 30 and 70, the mean of the tabular values for $n-1$ and $n+1$ may be taken. For larger values of n, the expression $2\chi^2 - 2n - 1$ may be used as a normal deviate with unit variance, remembering that the probability for χ^2 corresponds with that of a single tail of the normal curve.

a. n = degrees of freedom.

BIBLIOGRAPHY

Bailar, J. C., & Mosteller, F. (1988). Guidelines for statistical reporting in articles for medical journals. *Annals of Internal Medicine, 108,* 266-273.

Bates, E. S., & Abemayor, E. (1991). Slide presentation graphics using a personal computer. *Archives of Otolaryngology and Head and Neck Surgery, 117,* 1026-1030.

Braitman, L. (1991). Confidence intervals assess both clinical and statistical significance. *Annals of Internal Medicine, 114,* 515-517.

Campbell, D. T., & Stanley, J. C. (1963). *Experimental and quasi-experimental designs for research.* Chicago: Rand McNally.

Converse, J., & Presser, S. (1986). *Survey questions.* Beverly Hills, CA: Sage.

Dawson-Saunders, B., & Trapp, R. G. (1994). *Basic and clinical biostatistics* (2nd ed.). East Norwalk, CT: Appleton & Lange.

Fink, A. (1993). *Evaluation fundamentals: Guiding health programs, research, and policy.* Newbury Park, CA: Sage.

Fink, A. (Ed.). (1995). *A survey kit.* Thousand Oaks, CA: Sage.

 Contents of the kit:

 Fink, A. *The survey handbook.*

 Fink, A. *How to ask survey questions.*

 Bourque, L. B., & Fielder, E. P. *How to conduct self-administered and mail surveys.*

 Frey, J. H., & Oishi, S. M. *How to conduct interviews in person and on the telephone.*

 Litwin, M. *How to measure survey reliability and validity.*

 Fink, A. *How to analyze survey data.*

 Fink, A. *How to report on surveys.*

Fowler, F. J. (1993). *Survey research methods.* Newbury Park, CA: Sage.

Henry, G. T. (1990). *Practical sampling.* Newbury Park, CA: Sage.

Kraemer, H. C., & Thiemann, S. (1987). *How many subjects? Statistical power analysis in research.* Newbury Park, CA: Sage.

Pfeiffer, W. S. (1991). *Technical writing.* New York: Macmillan.

Siegel, S. (1956). *Nonparametric statistics for the behavioral sciences.* New York: McGraw-Hill.

Spinler, S. (1991). How to prepare and deliver pharmacy presentations. *American Journal of Hospital Pharmacy, 48,* 1730-1738.

INDEX

ABOUT THE AUTHORS

Arlene Fink, Ph.D., is Professor of Medicine and Professor of Public Health at the University of California, Los Angeles. She is on the Policy and Research Advisory Boards of UCLA's Robert Wood Johnson Clinical Scholars Program and President of Arlene Fink Associates and on the Boards of the Langley Research Institute and Market Tools. Her expertise includes health services research, program evaluation, survey research, and social and health science research methods. She has published in leading journals such as the *Journal of the American Medical Association,* the *New England Journal of Medicine,* and *Medical Care.* She has trained hundreds of health professionals, social scientists, and educators in research methods, program evaluation, and survey research. She has published more than 100 articles and monographs, including *Evaluation Fundamentals* and *The Survey Kit* (for Sage).

Jacqueline Kosecoff, Ph.D., is cofounder, President, and Co-Chief Executive Officer of Value Health Sciences, an applied health services research firm, and Adjunct Professor of Medicine and Public Health at the University of California, Los Angeles. Her areas of expertise include managed care, health services research, quality of care assessment, evaluation theory, technology assessment, disease management, and product development. She is a recognized expert in the area of quality of care assessment and has published in such journals as the *New England Journal of Medicine,* the *Journal of the American Medical Association, Lancet,* and the *Annals of Internal Medicine.* She is a consultant to the World Health Organization's Global Quality Assessment Program and serves on the Institute of Medicine's Board of Health Care Services and the RAND Graduate School's Board of Visitors.